This book belongs to

_____

...a woman after God's own heart.

Living with Passion & Purpose

Elizabeth George

HARVEST HOUSE PUBLISHERS
EUGENE, OREGON

Cover by Dugan Design Group, Bloomington, Minnesota

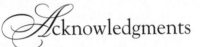

Acknowledgments

As always, thank you to my dear husband, Jim George, M.Div., Th.M., for your able assistance, guidance, suggestions, and loving encouragement on this project.

LIVING WITH PASSION AND PURPOSE
Copyright © 2005 Elizabeth George
Published by Harvest House Publishers
Eugene, Oregon 97402
www.harvesthousepublishers.com

ISBN 978-0-7369-0816-0 (pbk.)
ISBN 978-0-7369-3313-1 (eBook)

Printed in the United States of America

23 24 25 26 27 /BP-MS/ 20 19 18 17 16 15 14

Contents

Foreword

For some time I have been looking for Bible studies that I could use each day that would increase my knowledge of God's Word. In my search, I found myself struggling between two extremes: Bible studies that required little time but also had little substance, or studies that were in-depth and demanded more time than I could give. I discovered that I wasn't alone—there were many other women like me who were busy yet desired to spend quality time studying God's Word.

That's why I became excited when Elizabeth George shared her desire to create a series of women's Bible studies that offered in-depth lessons that could be completed in just 15-20 minutes per day. When she completed the first study—on Philippians—I was eager to try it out. I had already studied Philippians many times, but this was the first time I had come to understand exactly how the whole book fit together and how it can truly be lived out in my life. Each lesson was simple but insightful—and was written especially to apply to me as a woman!

In the Woman After God's Own Heart® Bible Study series, Elizabeth takes you step by step through the Scriptures, sharing wisdom she has gleaned from more than 20 years as a women's Bible teacher. The lessons are rich and meaningful because they're rooted in God's Word and have been lived out in Elizabeth's life. Her thoughtful and personable guidance makes you feel as though you are studying right alongside her—as if she is personally mentoring you in the greatest aspiration you could ever pursue: to become a woman after God's own heart.

If you're looking for Bible studies that can help you grow stronger in your knowledge of God's Word even in the most demanding of schedules, I know you'll find this series to be a welcome companion in your daily walk with God.

—LaRae Weikert
Vice President, Editorial,
Harvest House Publishers

Before You Begin

In my book *A Woman After God's Own Heart*®, I describe such a woman as one who ensures that God is first in her heart and the Ultimate Priority of her life. Then I share that one crucial way this desire can become reality is by nurturing a heart that abides in God's Word. To do so means that you and I must develop a root system anchored deep in God's Word.

Before you launch into this Bible study, take a moment to think about these aspects of a root system produced by the regular, faithful study of God's Word:

- *Roots are unseen*—You'll want to set aside time in solitude—"underground" if you will—to immerse yourself in God's Word and grow in Him.

- *Roots are for taking in*—Alone and with your Bible in hand, you'll want to take in and feed upon the truths of the Word of God and ensure your spiritual growth.

- *Roots are for storage*—As you form the habit of looking into God's Word, you'll find a vast, deep reservoir of divine hope and strength forming for the rough times.

- *Roots are for support*—Do you want to stand strong in the Lord? To stand firm against the pressures of life? The routine care of your roots through exposure to God's Word will cultivate you into a remarkable woman of endurance.

I'm glad you've chosen this study out of my A Woman After God's Own Heart® Bible study series. My prayer for you is that the truths you find in God's Word through this study will further transform your life into the image of His dear Son and empower you to be the woman you seek to be: a woman after God's own heart.

In His love,

Elizabeth George

Lesson 1

Setting the Stage

Luke 1

Prepare yourself to meet Jesus, the "Son of Man." As you read, keep in mind that this was Jesus' favorite term for Himself. Also realize this term was a prophetic reference to Messiah (see Daniel 7:13-14). As you study the Gospel of Luke, you'll run across this phrase 26 times.[1] More than that, Luke's gospel account gives particular attention to His humanity. Luke's writing is an accurate historical account (Luke 1:1-4) covering a period of about 35 years—from the birth of John the Baptist to the death and resurrection of Jesus. In it you'll see Jesus, the Perfect Man, the one and only true Representative of the whole human race.[2]

In addition you will enjoy many unique features in the longest of the four Gospels. For instance:

- Luke recounts the miraculous birth of the forerunner, John the Baptist.

- Luke alone writes of the boyhood of Jesus.

- Luke gives numerous references to women not found in the other gospels. (See Appendix on p. 152.)

- Luke centers more on prayer than the other Gospels.

- Luke gives special emphasis to the poor.

Finally, more than half the material found in the Gospel of Luke is not in any of the other three accounts, including 9 miracles, 13 parables, and a variety of messages and events.[3]

God's Message...

1. Read Luke 1:1-4. Who wrote this book of the Bible, and what was his purpose in writing this gospel?

2. Read Luke 1:5-25 concerning the first of two earth-shattering announcements. Who was the subject of the first announcement?

Who appeared to Elizabeth and Zacharias, and what was the announcement?

How did Zacharias respond, and what was the result?

Describe the ministry John would have (see also Luke 7:28).

3. Read Luke 1:26-38 concerning the second of two earth-shattering announcements. Who was the subject of the second announcement?

Note what you learn about Mary.

How did Mary respond, and what was the result?

What was prophesied to be the sign of the Savior's coming into the world in Isaiah 7:14?

What title was to be given to Jesus according to Luke 1:35?

4. Read Luke 1:39-56 and enjoy observing the sweet fellowship between two godly women. In a few words, describe their meeting.

What do you learn about Elizabeth in verse 36?

What do you learn about Mary in the following verses?

Verse 42—

Verse 47—

Verse 48—

Verses 46-55—

5. Read Luke 1:57-80 and briefly describe the events surrounding John's birth.

When was Zacharias's mouth opened (see also Luke 1:20)?

What did Zacharias prophesy about yet-to-be-born Jesus (verses 68-75)?

What did Zacharias prophesy about John (verses 76-79)?

...and Your Heart's Response

1. Think again about Luke 1. Note below the responses of each of the individuals in the story. Then share how each reaction instructs your heart.

   Luke in verse 3—

   Zacharias in verse 18—

   Mary in verse 38—

   Elizabeth in verse 42—

   Mary in verses 46-55—

   Zacharias in verses 67-79—

2. What is at least one truth or response you need to take away from Luke 1? Write it here, and record it on the chart in Lesson 25.

Living with Passion and Purpose

Passion is defined as "a strong feeling" and also as "an object of affection or enthusiasm." As God sets the stage for the arrival and appearance of His only begotten Son, we witness great passion in those who were involved in some way. Don't you think the same should be true of your feelings and affection and enthusiasm toward Jesus, your Savior, the Son of Man?

I love the words Mary used in her outpouring of worship for God concerning His Son. She marveled that "He who is mighty has done great things for me" (Luke 1:49). She let her passion be known. So did her cousin Elizabeth. And so did Zacharias...when his mouth was at last opened and his tongue loosed. The Bible says, "He spoke, praising God"!

Are you living out your passion for Jesus? And are you verbalizing that, helping to set the stage for Christ to dwell in the hearts of those who hear of Him from you? Or, put another way, are you living with passion? Are you walking the walk *and* talking the talk? Who can you share your passion for Jesus with today?

Responding to the Savior

Luke 2

ave you ever heard a group of elementary-school-age children reciting "the Christmas story" from Luke, chapter two? There's nothing like it! In fact, many adults can almost recite the story right along with them without even realizing they almost know it by heart. That's how familiar people are with the story of Jesus Christ's birth.

As you read through your Bible, you quickly notice that God is a seeking God. He sought out Adam after he sinned. He sought out Cain after the murder of Abel. Then followed Noah and Abraham, right on down through Bible history until we reach the events of the Christmas story, the ultimate seeking out of God to humanity.

We have already seen how two women, Mary and Elizabeth, responded in faith and obedience to God as He sought them, and how Zacharias initially responded in unbelief.

Now let's see how others responded as a seeking God moved forward on His plan for the salvation of mankind.

God's Message...

1. Read Luke 2:1-7. What moved Joseph and Mary to travel to Bethlehem, a rigorous and dangerous journey of 90 miles through hill country, despite Mary's pregnant condition?

What happened once they arrived there?

Share a few of the details surrounding the event.

What prophecy did this special set of circumstances fulfill from Micah 5:2 (see also John 7:42)?

2. Keeping in mind God's love for the poor, read Luke 2:8-20. Others were informed of the great thing that happened in Bethlehem. In verses 8-14, who was first to hear about the Savior, and how did they hear?

What was their response in verses 15-20?

What was the response of others who heard (verse 18)?

What was Mary's response (verse 19)?

3. Read Luke 2:21-24. What rituals took place in these scriptures?

Verse 21—

Verse 22—

Why were these rituals important according to verses 22-24 and 27?

4. Read Luke 2:25-38. How did Simeon respond to Jesus during His presentation in the temple in verses 28-35?

What key words did Simeon use to describe the infant?

How did Anna respond when she saw the baby Jesus in verse 38?

5. Read Luke 2:39-52. Although much of Jesus' early years are not mentioned in the Bible, the book of Luke tells us more than the other three Gospels. Make a brief list of what you learn about His growing-up years from these verses concerning:

His religious training at home—

His spiritual understanding—

His grasp of His purpose—

His relationship with His parents—

His growth and development—

What additional truths do these scriptures give about Jesus?

Galatians 4:4—

Galatians 4:5—

Hebrews 4:14-15—

...and Your Heart's Response

1. Think again about Luke 2. Note the responses of each of the following individuals. Then share how each reaction instructs your heart.

The shepherds in verses 15-20—

Simeon in verse 28—

Anna in verse 38—

Mary in verse 51—

Jesus in verse 51—

2. What is at least one truth or response you need to take away from Luke 2? Write it here, and record it in Lesson 25.

Living with Passion and Purpose

I believe a Christian woman's heart for God should be like a tea kettle on a flaming stove burner—hot to the touch, visibly steaming, and audible. You see, she's excited. Her heart is hot. The heat of her love moves her to activity. And her passion for Christ—the object of her affection and enthusiasm—finds a voice. Everyone within earshot hears about the great things He who is mighty has done for her (Luke 1:49).

Think about your heart for a minute. How audible is your passion for Jesus? And how intense is the heat of your love for Him? The presence of the Savior should inspire a fervent reaction in your soul…just like it did in the shepherds, in Simeon, and in Anna. These believers verbalized and shared their passion—and the good news!—with others. Does your passion for the Son of Man show? Is it known by others? Are you, like the shepherds, glorifying and praising God for all that you know and have heard? Are you, like Simeon, blessing God with your every breath for His salvation? And are you, like dear Anna, giving thanks and telling others about the Lord Jesus? Are others hearing of your passion for Christ?

Lesson 3

Beginning in Ministry

I've heard it said, "Success is when preparation meets opportunity." Preparation gives you and me the ability to seize opportunities as they present themselves. That's what happened in my ministry life. During my private years at home—years of ministry devoted to raising my children, supporting a busy pastor-husband, and running a busy home—I sought to prepare myself and grow in my Christian life. Then one day, when my children were older a different kind of ministry opportunity—for a more public ministry—came along. Our church needed women to teach in a newly formed women's ministry. Because I had spent those years in preparation, I hesitantly volunteered my services...and, in God's timing and great grace, that teaching ministry developed into a writing ministry.

As we come to chapter 3 of Luke, we encounter a similar scenario. Both John the Baptist and Jesus had spent close to

30 years preparing for the days when they would begin their ministries. Then John began preaching in the wilderness, and Jesus began by fulfilling the law of God by being baptized. Thirty years of preparation by God equipped both of these men for service. They show us that, if we desire ministries to others, we must start with preparation...and then wait for God to provide the opportunities.

God's Message...

1. Read Luke 3:1-2. Jot down the names of the great leaders of Jesus' day and some information about them.

   And yet, what happened in verse 2?

   What was John the Baptist doing at this time in his life? How does Matthew 3:4 describe him?

   How did John describe himself in John 1:23?

2. Read Luke 3:3-20. List some of the details that distinguish:

   John's ministry—

John's message—

3. Read Luke 3:21-22 (see also John 1:29-34). Note all that happened in these verses.

What was the significance of this event to:

Jesus Himself—

John—

The people present—

Why was Jesus baptized, according to Matthew 3:13-15?

4. Read Luke 3:23-38. As you begin reading, note Jesus' age—the number of years He had been in preparation, so to speak, for His public ministry.

Scan through Luke's genealogy of Jesus, the listing of His generations of human descent through His mother, Mary, as the Son of Man. With whom does Jesus' genealogy begin (verse 38)?

What name substantiates His royal lineage (verse 31)?

...and Your Heart's Response

1. Think again about Luke 3. What impresses you about:

John's ministry—

Jesus' baptism—

Jesus' genealogy—

2. What is at least one truth or response you need to take away from Luke 3? Write it here, and record it in Lesson 25.

Living with Passion and Purpose

It was at age 30 that Jesus began His public ministry, to more actively move toward fulfilling the purpose of His life. Jesus certainly did not wait until age 30 to bless and to serve others. Many Christians, however, wait to serve or, worse yet, fail to ever begin preparing to minister to the body of Christ. To live with passion and purpose means we should be aggressively taking advantage of each day to not only help others, but to also gear up for greater things, to spend time in preparation so that we are ready when greater opportunities to serve our Lord present themselves. What can you do today to prepare for ministry? And what can you do today to better the lives of others?

Lesson 4

Handling Temptation

Luke 4

I'm sure you've noticed that every day is loaded with trials and temptations. "The devil made me do it!" is a common excuse given by many when trying to explain away some sin or failure. However, this is not exactly a true statement, as Luke shows us in this upcoming chapter. In actuality, as has been quipped, "We start the fire, and the devil supplies the gasoline."

But in the opening verses of Luke 4, when Jesus was assaulted by the crafty wiles of the devil, we see a different picture. Follow along and see how Jesus never allowed the fire to start nor the devil to supply the gasoline! Note how Jesus was tested, fought the battle, handled temptation, won the victory, and went on in the power of the Holy Spirit to mightily teach the truth and wondrously display His authority.

God's Message...

1. Read Luke 4:1-13. Who led Jesus into the wilderness, for what purpose, and for how long?

   Jesus' temptations were real. In each instance, Jesus was tempted to act independently of the Father's provision. What was the first temptation Satan used to test Jesus, and how did Jesus respond (verses 3-4)?

   What was the second temptation Satan used to test Jesus, and how did He respond (verses 5-8)?

   What was the third temptation Satan used to test Jesus, and how did He respond (verses 9-12)?

   As a point of information, be aware that between verses 13 and 14 about one year of Jesus' ministry in Jerusalem and Judea took place (see John 2:12–4:1). Because of this early ministry, the "news...went out," even to the remote areas of Galilee, such as Nazareth.

2. Read Luke 4:14-30. Upon completing the time of testing in the wilderness and the early ministry, Jesus returned to His hometown of Nazareth. What Old Testament prophecy did He claim to fulfill (see Isaiah 61:1-2)?

How did the people respond to Jesus' message, and why, according to John 8:37?

3. Read Luke 4:31-37. Here Jesus began to show forth His deity and His authority over every realm of nature. Briefly describe Christ's first act and what it demonstrated about His authority.

4. Read Luke 4:38-40. Briefly describe Christ's acts and what they demonstrated about His authority.

5. Read Luke 4:41-44. Briefly describe Christ's acts and what they again demonstrated about His authority.

6. Read Luke 4:42-44. What was the crowd's response to Jesus' mighty acts?

...and Your Heart's Response

1. Why did Jesus have to be tested, according to:

Hebrews 2:17-18—

Hebrews 4:15—

What do you learn about using the Scriptures to handle temptation, and how can this help you the next time you are tested? (See also 1 John 2:15-17.)

How do these verses encourage you?

1 Corinthians 10:13—

Ephesians 6:13-17—

Hebrews 4:14-16—

2. Note again how busy Jesus was throughout Luke 4. Yet what do we witness Him doing in verse 42?

How is this a good example for you to follow in your life? In your ministry?

3. Jesus was a man on a mission, a man who understood His purpose (see verses 18-19 and 43). This affected all His activities and His relationships. How does His example encourage you to live with greater passion and purpose?

4. What is at least one truth or response you need to take away from Luke 4? Write it here, and record it in Lesson 25.

Living with Passion and Purpose

Having a purpose, a goal, is one of the most dynamic forces in human nature. With purpose, a man or woman can accomplish amazing feats, achieve challenging goals, and persist through staggering difficulties. But without purpose, many men and women drift through life with little to show for their existence.

Do you yet know your purpose? Your reason for being? The course of your direction at each fresh sunrise? Joshua knew his purpose. He declared, "As for me and my house, we will serve the Lord" (Joshua 24:15). Mary knew her purpose. She said, "Behold the maidservant of the Lord! Let it be to me according to your word" (Luke 1:38). Paul knew his purpose. He proclaimed, "For to me, to live is Christ" (Philippians 1:21). Ask God and others to help you understand and focus on God's grand purpose for your life, all the while remembering that God desires that you remain pure (1 Thessalonians 4:3-5), and that, with God's help, you can handle temptation.

Following Jesus

 he crowds were beginning to gather. And, as Jesus faithfully ministered to the multitudes, He was on the lookout for people of passion and purpose, those who would be willing to make sacrifices in order to follow Him as their Master, those who would count the cost and follow Him. The crowds would come, and eventually they would go. But in the ebb and flow of the throng, a few chose to count the cost and follow Jesus.

We are learning much about Jesus, but in Luke 5 we learn what it means to *follow* Jesus. Four simple men offered all they had to Jesus, forsaking all to follow Him. In the end, God used them mightily to extend Jesus' ministry to the ends of the earth.

God's Message...

1. Read Luke 5:1-11. How does the scene begin, and yet where does Jesus turn His attention?

   Genesaret — to fishermen

   As Jesus performed yet another miracle, how was His authority once again demonstrated? *Lots of fish*

   Describe how the fishermen's attitudes and actions toward Jesus changed. *Fell on their knees*

   In this passage Jesus called men to follow Him. According to Mark 1:16-19, who were these first four disciples? List them here and what you learn about them.

   — *James*

   — *John*

   — *Simon*

   — *Andrew*

2. Read Luke 5:12-26. As Jesus' ministry increased, so did the numbers of people who came to see and hear Him. Briefly describe the healing in verses 12-15 and the results.

Briefly describe the healing in verses 18-26 and the results. What authority did Jesus demonstrate in verse 24?

Power to heal

3. Read Luke 5:27-39. What was Jesus' call to the hated tax collector, and how did he respond?

Follow me

Write the name of this fifth disciple called by Jesus. (See also Matthew 9:9 for his Greek name.)

Note the confrontations that occurred during the dinner. Describe how Jesus responded to the questions regarding:

Spending time with sinners— *Called them to repent.*

John the Baptist and his followers versus Jesus and His followers—

Jesus used a parable to illustrate the significance of His ministry over that of those who had gone before Him. What analogies did He use in verses 36-38?

No new cloth on Old:
New wine skin

What would be the response of some to this "new wine" (verse 39)? *They wouldn't like it*

…and Your Heart's Response

1. How did the four fishermen in Luke 5:2-11 indicate their willingness to follow Jesus?

How does this instruct your heart regarding your commitment to follow Jesus? *Priorities*

2. Faith is required to follow Jesus. How was faith in Jesus revealed in:

The leper— *He had faith to be healed.*

The paralytic and his friends— *He also knew he would be healed.*

How is your faith in Christ being revealed today?

Be an example

3. How did Jesus' choice of the hated and despised tax collector evidence:

Jesus' love for outcasts and sinners— *He wanted them to follow Him Luke 19:10*

Jesus' foreknowledge of a person's potential— *Acts 15:8 Heb. 4:12*

What did he do to share his faith in Jesus with others?

He had a big party. —

List several people you know who need to hear about Jesus, and describe what you plan to do to share the good news of the gospel with them.

4. What is at least one truth or response you need to take away from Luke 5? Write it here, and record it in Lesson 25. *Be Compassionate.*

Living with Passion and Purpose

Christians love to sing about following Jesus, about going with Him all the way. But following the Lord is no easy task or light commitment. Jesus is a loving but demanding Master. He expects His followers to listen, learn, and obey.

When Jesus, at a later time in His ministry, taught about being the bread of life (see John 6:41-58), many of His fair-weather followers began to leave. They could not accept His teaching, so He watched them depart.

Are you one who hesitates, rationalizes, and says, "This is a hard saying" (John 6:60) whenever Jesus speaks? Or do you say along with Peter, "Lord, to whom shall we go? You have the words of eternal life" (John 6:68)? To live with passion and purpose you must, like Peter, James, John, Andrew, and Levi, follow Jesus wholeheartedly.

Learning How to Live

Luke 6

*I*f you're like many people, there just aren't enough hours in your day! As you look at your to-do list, you know before you begin that today is simply not going to be long enough to get it all done! Does Jesus ever have a message for His busy women! In His perfect wisdom, He shows us the value of foresight, prayer, preparation, and priorities in making sure what is truly important gets done.

As we begin combing through Luke 6, Jesus' ministry was about half over. By human standards, His ministry was a success—crowds, followers, and a number of faithful disciples. But our Lord knew time was growing short. In a few months He would set His face toward Jerusalem and the cross (see Luke 9:51). Who would continue the ministry after Jesus' departure?

After praying all night, Jesus shifted the focus of His time and ministry. He selected 12 men to personally train, men who would later be sent forth as His apostles, His "sent ones." Let's follow the process of discipleship as Jesus taught His new ambassadors how to live in a new world order—the kingdom of God.

God's Message...

1. Read Luke 6:1-5. Describe the first Sabbath-day scene.

   Where did it occur? *Grain field*

   Who was present? *Pharisees - disciples & Jesus*

   What Old Testament law did the Pharisees think Jesus and His disciples were supposedly breaking (see Exodus 20:10)? *Working on Sabbath*

   How did Jesus answer His accusers and assert His authority as the Son of Man?

   Rebuked them

2. Read Luke 6:6-11. Describe the second Sabbath-day scene.

   Where did it occur? *Synagog*

   Who was present? *Jesus, Scribes & pharisees*

   What Old Testament law was Jesus supposedly breaking (see Exodus 20:10)? *Work on Sabbath*

   How did Jesus answer His accusers?

How did they respond to Jesus' answer?

rage

3. Read Luke 6:12-16. How does this section begin?

List here the 12 disciples Jesus chose to be with Him and any additional information given about them. Star or check those you have already met in Luke's Gospel.

— Simon   — Philip

— Andrew   — Judas Is

— James   — Matthew

— John   — James Thaddeus

— Thomas   — Bartholomew

— Simon   .   — Judas

4. Read Luke 6:17-49. These teachings from Jesus are generally referred to as The Beatitudes. Who was present? And why?

Create a brief checklist of the contents of The Beatitudes (verses 20-26).

Who was blessed...   ...and why?

- *Poor*
- *Hungry*
- *Sad*
- *reviled*

Who was warned...   ...and why?

- *Rich*
- *Full*
- *Those who LOL*
- *False prophets*

In a few words, what did Jesus teach regarding:

Loving your enemies (verses 27-36)—

Harshly judging others (verses 37-42)—

Don't do it

Fruit in the lives of others (verses 43-45)—

OK to be a fruit Inspector

Building on the truth (verses 46-49)—

...and Your Heart's Response

1. Volumes have been written on the contents of Luke 6. As you seek to digest the many elements of this chapter, list three lessons you want to remember to apply from Jesus' life and actions.

   — *Always lean towards mercy*
   — *Don't be judgemental*

   —

2. List at least three lessons you should remember to apply from Jesus' teachings.

   — *Be careful of what goes into your ♡ as it will come out*
   — *Love the enemy.*

   —

3. How do you think Jesus' habit of prayer (see Luke 3:21; 5:16; 6:12) could help you to:

   Focus on God's purposes— *Not self*

   Make better choices—

   Live out Jesus' teachings—

4. What is at least one truth or response you need to take away from Luke 6? Write it here, and record it in Lesson 25.

Living with Passion and Purpose

If you have ever read through the four Gospels in the New Testament, no doubt you have heard of Jesus' famous Sermon on the Mount. In fact, some have asked, Are the teachings of Jesus here in Luke 6:20-49 a part of that well-loved sermon? While Luke's sermon contains similarities to the full sermon in Matthew 5–7, it is also possible that, like all good teachers, Jesus may have given similar teachings on various occasions.

But whether Luke's information was a part of the better-known sermon or not, the important thing is that the apostles were the recipients of Jesus' teaching. These men were being groomed by the Lord for a worldwide ministry. They needed to glimpse and grasp their purpose so that one day, when the time was right, their Holy Spirit-infused passion (Acts 4:8 and 4:31) would thrust them into a fearless ministry of boldly proclaiming the good news of the risen Savior.

As you leave the teachings of your Savior here in Luke 6, pray that any lost vision or passion will be rekindled by what you have learned from Jesus about how to live as a woman after God's own heart.

esson 7

Touching Lives

ave you ever stopped to think about how many kinds of people God sends to cross your path and how many kinds of needs they represent? Whether they are your little and big family members, neighbors, strangers in a store or on the street, or those you know through the church prayer chain, opportunity is never lacking!

Well, however busy and packed your days are with people in need, Jesus' days were even more so. In this one chapter, Luke 7, we see Jesus spending His days ministering not to those who seemed by human standards to be most worthy but to those who needed Him most—a slave who was sick, a dead only son of a widow, a grieving mother, a disheartened prophet, and a fallen woman. All had needs, and the Son of Man responded to them.

In Isaiah 7:14 the prophet predicted that a virgin would

.bear a son and His name would be Immanuel, meaning "God with us." As you'll witness firsthand in Luke 7, this prediction was certainly fulfilled in the life of the Perfect Man. The people saw Jesus' loving concern in action, and they glorified God and said, "A great prophet has risen up among us" and, "God has visited His people" (verse 16). Yes, Immanuel was among His creation, touching lives in a big way!

God's Message...

1. Read Luke 7:1-10. Upon finishing His great sermon, Jesus returned to His center of activities in Capernaum. But His ministry continued. What request came to Jesus from a Roman centurion, and through whom?

   Come heal my servant.

   How did the centurion express his unworthiness?

   He sent friends to tell Jesus not to come to his home.

   How did he acknowledge Jesus' authority? *Just speak it and I know you can heal him.*

   What impressed Jesus most about the soldier, and what was the end result? *He found him faithful the servant was healed.*

2. Read Luke 7:11-17. As Jesus neared the village of Nain, what occurred? *A crying widow with many people around her! Men carrying her dead son.*

   What was Jesus' response to a poor grieving widow who had lost her only son; and what authority did He demonstrate? *He had Compassion on her*

How did the people respond?   *They had fear.*

3. Read again Luke 3:19-20 and then read Luke 7:18-35.
Where was John the Baptist?   *Prison*

What did John have his disciples ask Jesus?   *If he
was the one.*

How did Jesus "answer" before He spoke a verbal message to be given to John?   *Go tell him all you
have seen & heard. How the blind
see, etc.*

Read Isaiah 35:5-6 and 61:1. John the Baptist knew of
these prophecies. How would Jesus' actions have com-
forted John concerning his doubts?   *He fulfilled
prophecies.*

Briefly describe John as pictured by Jesus in Luke 7:24-
28.   *A simple man, not rich by any
means.*   *Ɨ 61:1*

4. Read Luke 7:36-50. While Jesus was dining, who
approached Him, and what did she do?   *A woman
She took her ointment and washed Jesus
feet with her tears, etc.*

What did Simon, the Pharisee, conclude?   *He who gave more - was more appreciative
of being forgiven.*

How did Jesus handle Simon's reasoning?   *She gave more because she was forgiven
more.*

How did He handle the woman's repentance?
*He said her faith saved her. Go
in peace.*

...and Your Heart's Response

1. Who do you know that needs the Savior, and in what ways can you call upon Jesus to assist them? *Eric .*
Be a witness and help .

2. What is your usual response to those who are suffering, and what qualities from Jesus do you need to emulate when you encounter someone in distress? *Be compassionate.*

3. Write out Romans 3:23 here. *For all have sinned and come short of the glory of God !*

Write out Romans 6:23 here. *For the wages of sin is death. But the gift of God is eternal life through Jesus Christ our Lord.*
Read again Luke 7:50. Have your sins been forgiven by Jesus Christ? Please explain your answer. *Amen !*

4. As you review the content of Luke 7, in what ways do you see Jesus' compassion for people revealed?
Blind see, lame walk, lepers cleansed, deaf hear, dead are raised , the gospel is preached .

5. What is at least one truth or response you need to take away from Luke 7? Write it here, and record it in Lesson 25. *Be faithful*

Living with Passion and Purpose

Our world is full of needy people—people who are hurting physically, mentally, and spiritually. Many come to us with outstretched hands and hearts. Our response should be to passionately reach out with compassion and touch those who are in need of the love of Christ with the love of Christ. It is as we show forth Christ's love that others are shown the way to the Savior. In light of the biblical commands that appear on page 47, may our prayer be, "Lord, who can I reach out to and touch today?"

Be kindly affectionate to one another with brotherly love, in honor giving preference to one another; not lagging in diligence, fervent in spirit, serving the Lord; rejoicing in hope, patient in tribulation, continuing steadfastly in prayer; distributing to the needs of the saints, given to hospitality.

ROMANS 12:10-13

Let nothing be done through selfish ambition or conceit, but in lowliness of mind let each esteem others better than himself. Let each of you look out not only for his own interests, but also for the interests of others.

PHILIPPIANS 2:2-4

The end of all things is at hand; therefore be serious and watchful in your prayers. And above all things, have fervent love for one another, for "love will cover a multitude of sins." Be hospitable to one another without grumbling. As each one has received a gift, minister it to one another, as good stewards of the manifold grace of God.

1 PETER 4:7-10

Lesson 8

Submitting to Authority

Luke 8

Oh, is the biblical teaching on wives submitting to their husbands ever a battlefield! Yet over and over we read in the Bible about submission to all kinds of authority. Recognizing and submitting to authority is no easy assignment. That's because people basically want to be in control of their lives and circumstances...at least until a crisis comes along.

As you'll see throughout Luke 8, Jesus shows us that His divine control over all things ensures that we can trust Him with our lives and all its ups and downs. The four miracles recorded in this chapter reveal the authority the Son of Man has over nature, demons, disease, and death. Don't wait until the boat is sinking to recognize and submit to His authority. Submit now and marvel at the ministry of the Son of Man in your life.

God's Message...

1. Read Luke 8:1-3, keeping in mind that Luke 8 shows us many instances of Jesus' ministry. What was the focus and extent of Jesus' ministry?

   List the people mentioned in these verses and how they are described.

   What was the ministry of the women who followed Jesus? (Remember Luke, more than the other Gospels, highlights the positive role that women played in Jesus' public ministry. See appendix on p. 152.)

2. Read Luke 8:4-18. Jesus' teaching ministry often involved using parables or stories. Briefly sum up the teaching of His "Parable of the Soils."

   The first soil—

   The second soil—

   The third soil—

   The fourth soil—

Briefly sum up the teaching of Jesus' "Parable of the Lamp."

What is the instruction in verse 18?

In Luke 8:19-21, whom did Jesus consider to be His true family?

3. Read Luke 8:22-25. Regardless of how close the disciples were to Jesus, they were still in need of His ministry. Describe the scene here.

What did the disciples say to the Master?

In what ways did He answer them?

4. Read Luke 8:26-39. Who was on the receiving end of Jesus' ministry here? Briefly describe what happened.

How did the man respond to Jesus' miracle, and what instruction did Jesus give him?

How did the people respond?

List a few things taught here about demons.

5. Read Luke 8:40-56. List the people mentioned in these verses, how they are described, and how they differ from one another.

In both cases, what did Jesus do that:

Demonstrated His passion and concern for mankind—

Demonstrated that He was the Christ, the Son of the living God—

...and Your Heart's Response

1. Luke tells of the contributions women made to the ministry of Jesus. What "assistance" can you give the Master for His ministry?

2. No one can be neutral about the truth of God. Which soil in Luke 8:5-18 pictures your life? Why?

As you think about verse 21, how do you measure up? Are there any areas in which you are not obeying the Word of God? If so, what will you do about it?

3. The believer who grows exceedingly fearful during the storms of life reveals that his or her faith is focused where it shouldn't be. In what way was the disciples' faith defective, as shown in verses 22-25?

What can you learn from their failure as you face the storms in your life?

What instruction do these scriptures offer?

Psalm 69:15-16—

Psalm 116:3-4—

4. Think about your ministry at home. How can you declare to those in your family and at home what great things Jesus has done and is doing for you (Luke 8:39)?

In what ways do you think your ministry at home is important?

5. What qualities do you witness in Jesus' attitudes and actions in verses 41-56?

Which one instructs you most? And why?

6. What is at least one truth or response you need to take away from Luke 8? Write it here, and record it in Lesson 25.

Living with Passion and Purpose

One of the most heartwarming accounts in the Gospels comes in this chapter regarding the life of a demon-possessed man. Alone, without family, he was in a hopeless condition. But miracle of miracles, Jesus commanded the unclean spirits to leave the man's body. As a result, he was healed, calmed, and clothed, and then he sat at the feet of Jesus.

But the story doesn't end there. Submitting to the authority of Jesus, he returned to his home with a purpose. He was to "tell what great things God has done for you" (Luke 8:39). And what about his passion? "He went his way and proclaimed throughout the whole city what great things Jesus had done for him" (verse 39).

Are you faithfully following through on one of your purposes, that of telling others what God has done for you? Ask God to revitalize your passion for telling others about what Jesus has done in your life.

Lesson 9

Counting the Cost

Luke 9

on't you hate dealing with a high-pressure salesman? If you're like me, you get flustered. You can't think. You feel intimidated...and usually make a bad decision and end up with something you didn't want or don't like afterward.

Well, Jesus was definitely not a high-pressure salesman. In fact, His methods ran in the opposite direction. He asked people to count the cost of following Him. Aside from the command "Follow Me," Jesus repeated the statement "Whoever loses His life for My sake" more times in the Gospels than any other saying.[4]

Jesus was not looking for those who would follow Him when it was convenient. Instead, He was looking for those who would count the cost and follow, no matter what sacrifices were needed up front and along the way. The roll call of Jesus' followers is convicting and thought provoking!

For instance, John the Baptist was beheaded. The boy in the multitude gave up his sack lunch of bread and fish. The disciples took up the cross and suffered disgrace and death.

And Jesus calls you and me to do likewise. We must sacrifice our pride, possessions, arrogance, and selfishness. And we must give up our excuses, too! Following Jesus requires sacrifice. Therefore, He demands that we count the cost.

God's Message...

1. Read Luke 9:1-10. How did Jesus further extend His ministry, and through whom?

   What authority did Jesus pass on to these men?

   Briefly describe what happened.

2. Read Luke 9:11-17. As Jesus withdrew with the apostles, what happened, and how did He handle it?

   How did Jesus' attitude and that of the apostles differ?

3. Read Luke 9:18-62. Time was passing and Jesus began to reveal more about Himself. What did Jesus seek to divulge to His disciples (verses 18-22 and 43-45) about:

Who He was—

What His future involved—

What is required of those who would truly follow Jesus:

In verses 23-26—

In verses 57-62—

What miracle occurred in verses 28-36, and what did it reveal about Jesus?

What miracle occurred in verses 37-42, and what did it reveal about Jesus?

What is required of those who would truly be great (verses 46-48)?

In Luke 9:51-56, how is what Jesus had revealed about His future beginning to come true? Briefly describe what happened.

...and Your Heart's Response

1. As you reflect on Luke 9:1-10, what leadership principles do you learn from Jesus?

2. Once again, what do you witness of Jesus' passion and compassion for people in verses 11-17?

   What do you think He was trying to teach and demonstrate to His disciples?

   What do you learn from Jesus' example and the disciples' wrong attitude?

3. Review verses 23-26 and 57-62. How will you "deny" yourself and "follow" Jesus today?

   Write out Jesus' principle of greatness found in verse 48. How can you act on this principle today?

4. What is at least one truth or response you need to take away from Luke 9? Write it here, and record it in Lesson 25.

Living with Passion and Purpose

I'm sure you've discovered along the path of your life that no success comes without sacrifice. Ask any champion athlete or concert musician what they had to give up in order to attain their level of expertise, and, somewhere in their explanation, you will hear that they counted the cost and made the necessary daily sacrifices.

It's no different in your Christian life. Jesus freely let people leave who were not willing to pay the price of following Him. He cautioned one would-be follower after he gave Jesus an excuse, "No one, having put his hand to the plow, and looking back, is fit for the kingdom of God" (Luke 9:62). A true follower of Christ must count the cost of commitment initially...but it doesn't stop there. Becoming a disciple of Christ is not merely a one-time transaction. Jesus was asking His followers—and is asking you!—to count the cost on a daily basis as you live for Him. Catch the passion and purpose in this C.T. Studd saying:

> "Only one life, 'twill soon be past,
> only what's done for Christ will last."

esson 10

Serving the Lord

ow do you handle rejection? Do you withdraw in fear? Do you drop off the scene? Do you find yourself cowering in corners, keeping a low profile? Do you clam up and say nothing from that time onward?

We can all learn from Jesus how to better handle rejection. What did He do when He sensed the initial tide of popularity turning and the scent of rejection in the air? Answer: He boldly and methodically multiplied His ministry. He intensified the actions that would benefit and enhance His purpose. He went into high gear. For the Son of Man there would be no quiet disappearing act or giving up of His purpose. See for yourself and learn from the Master how to continue serving God *after* a setback.

God's Message...

1. Read Luke 10:1-16. How do you continue to see Jesus' expanding and extending His ministry here (verse 1)?

   List some of the instructions Jesus gave this group.

   What authority did He give them in verse 9?

   How did Jesus prepare this group for some of the realities of serving Him in verse 16?

2. Read Luke 10:17-24. What appears to have excited Jesus' representatives most?

   How did Jesus correct their focus concerning the supreme cause for serving and for rejoicing (verse 20)?

3. Read Luke 10:25-37, known as "The Parable of the Good Samaritan," recorded only by Luke. What initial question was put forth to Jesus, and how did Jesus reply?

How did the lawyer answer Jesus' question?

What second question did the lawyer pose?

Briefly summarize Jesus' answer in verses 30-35. Be sure to contrast the response of the two religious leaders—the priest and the Levite—and that of the good Samaritan.

How did Jesus end this encounter with the lawyer?

Jesus' question—

The lawyer's answer—

Jesus' instruction—

What was Jesus' message about service to this man and to those listening (and reading)?

4. Read Luke 10:38-42. Describe the following:

The scene—

Those present—

Martha—

Mary—

What do you learn here about:

Service—

The limits of service—

The importance of worship—

...and Your Heart's Response

1. As you consider the great harvest (verse 2), what is your
   great responsibility?

   What does 2 Corinthians 5:18-20 say an aspect of our service or ministry is to be?

   In this chapter, Jesus intensified His outreach to unbe-
   lievers. In what ways will you intensify your witnessing
   this week?

2. Read James 2:14-18. As you think again about "The Parable of the Good Samaritan," why—according to Jesus and James—are good deeds important?

The lawyer in Luke 10:25-37 knew the Old Testament teachings well. What does Micah 6:8 say is required of those who know God?

Read James 1:22-25. How did the lawyer, with all his knowledge of the Law and the Scriptures, fail?

How about you? Are there areas in which you need change and improvement based on what is revealed in the mirror of God's Word, the Bible?

Take an inventory of your mercy toward those in need. How can you be a better "neighbor" to others?

3. Do you most resemble Martha or Mary in Luke 10:38-42? Explain your answer.

What new choices, changes, or improvements must be made in your life?

4. What is at least one truth or response you need to take away from Luke 10? Write it here, and record it in Lesson 25.

Living with Passion and Purpose

Mary and Martha—why do many love them so much? Because at times one can identify with both of them! Many are women after God's own heart, women on a mission, whether that mission is planning a dinner party, home-schooling our children, making the carpool rounds, running a busy household, organizing a ministry, or a business. But with such pressure and intense focus and purposed service, it's easy to lose sight of the need for passionate worship. Yes, purpose and momentum are needed. We must be Marthas at times. But, like Mary, we must pause in our hectic schedules and commune with the Lord. Active service is needed...but so is personal worship. When we take time to worship, we discover that communion with God is the starting place—and the sustainer—of all our service for God and for others.

Living Godly in an Ungodly World

Luke 11

*I*f you are involved in any witnessing efforts, I'm sure you have seen a variety of negative reactions as well as positive, to the truth about Jesus Christ. But don't give up! Instead, be encouraged, because Jesus experienced reactions to His message—and to Himself!—as He preached and worked miracles and sought to redeem sinners. In Luke 11 you will observe several of Jesus' confrontations. For instance, one group accused Him of being associated with the devil, while another group sat on the fence, waiting for yet another miraculous sign.

As you read along, you will notice that there is an all-out battle being waged between good and evil, between God and Satan. You'll also comprehend that there is no middle ground when it comes to following Christ: a person is either striving to be godly, or giving in to ungodliness. So what can we do? Jesus tells us. We can pray...and we can take a firm stand for Christ, because, when it comes to Jesus, there is no neutrality allowed! Jesus said, "He who is not with Me, is against me" (Luke 11:23).

God's Message...

1. Read Luke 11:1-4. As stated in the beginning of this study, Luke records more about prayer and the prayer life of Jesus than any other Gospel writer. How does this scene open?

   What did Jesus' disciples want to know, and how did He respond?

   Write out the following elements in Jesus' model prayer:

   Our relationship with God—

   Our worship—

   Our desire for God's will—

   Our dependence on God—

   Our confession of sin—

Our weakness and need for God's help—

2. Read Luke 11:5-13. What was the point of Jesus' "Parable of the Persistent Friend"?

What was the point of Jesus' "Parable of the Good Father"?

What do these parables teach us about prayer?

Parable #1—

Parable #2—

3. Read Luke 11:14-36. How did the leadership of Israel handle their dilemma of explaining Jesus' miracles?

Briefly note the many ways Jesus refuted their reasoning, silenced their accusations, and refused their demands for a sign:

Verses 17-20—

Verses 21-22—

Verses 24-26—

Verses 29-32—

Verses 33-36—

4. Read Luke 11:37-54. What did Jesus do as a result of the leaders' increased and open rejection of Him as God's Messiah for Israel?

...and Your Heart's Response

1. After looking at Jesus' pattern for prayer, what elements do you realize are missing from your prayers that need your immediate attention?

2. What from Luke 11:5-13 makes the greatest impression on you about your prayer life? Why?

3. Jesus chastised the leaders of Israel because their inner life differed from the image they portrayed (verses 39-52). In what ways or areas is the same true of your inner life, and how can you strive for godliness?

4. What is at least one truth or response you need to take away from Luke 11? Write it here, and record it in Lesson 25.

Living with Passion and Purpose

As I looked again at this lesson and at the title of our study, I realized that Luke 11 is about *praying* with passion and *living* with purpose. As the chapter opens, we see Jesus praying. There's no doubt that Jesus lived with a fiery passion. His disciples were reminded daily of His zeal as they watched His tireless ministry to people. Where, they may have wondered, did it come from? And yet one answer was obvious—His habit of prayer seemed to nurture His zeal.

Do you long for more passion in your Christian life, to be more godly, more like Jesus? Then do as the disciples did. Ask Jesus to teach you to pray. And, as you steadily make prayer the habit of your life, you'll discover God's purpose for your life. As you pray, your days will become pointed rather than pointless, full rather than empty, hopeful rather than hopeless, vibrant rather than lifeless. Can prayer do all of this? Try it and find out for yourself!

Lesson 12

Getting Right with God

Have you ever wondered about the origin of some of the words you use? Every word in the English language has a history. Take, for instance, the word *hypocrite*. It comes from the Greek language and originally meant "to play-act" or "to wear a mask." In ancient Greece, during drama performances, an actor would put on different masks to play a variety of characters on the stage. Each time he put on a new mask, the actor would "pretend" to be a different person—this made him a "hypocrite." In Jesus' day, as in our day, a hypocrite is someone who outwardly pretends to be one person, while inwardly he or she is someone entirely different.

In this chapter, Luke shows Jesus continuing His straightforward teaching on the standards God sets for those who would be kingdom citizens. Hypocrisy was at the top of

Jesus' list of vile sins. Look now as we hold our lives and conduct up to the light of God's Word.

God's Message...

1. Read Luke 12:1-12, keeping in mind the universal sin of hypocrisy, even in Christians. Here, Jesus continued His condemnation of the Pharisees for their hypocrisy. What had the Jewish lawyers done to merit this final—and terrible—condemnation?

   Read Luke 11:39 again. How had Jesus already referred to the hypocrisy of the Pharisees?

2. Read Luke 12:13-34. What warning did Jesus give regarding covetousness and materialism in verses 13-15?

   What is the message of "The Parable of the Rich Fool," recorded only in Luke's gospel?

   What does a wise person do with riches (verses 31-34)?

3. Read Luke 12:35-40. How does Jesus' imagery of a wedding feast encourage watchfulness?

4. Read Luke 12:41-48. What was Peter's question?

What was Jesus' answer concerning the need for faithfulness?

5. Read Luke 12:49-53. What did Jesus say His coming would produce (verse 51)?

6. Read Luke 12:54-59. What were the people able to discern?

Yet what were they unable to discern?

What would be the consequence if there were no change in the people's discernment, according to verses 57-59?

...and Your Heart's Response

1. As you think over Jesus' message about covetousness, anxiety, and the watchful expectation of His return, how should His instructions affect the content of your witnessing and message to others?

What is a proper biblical attitude toward possessions, according to:

Luke 12:13-23—

1 Timothy 6:7-10—

1 John 2:15-17—

2. According to Luke 12:35-48, how can we be ready for Jesus' return?

3. Luke 12:49-59 continues to focus on Jesus' return and His offer of salvation. What will His return mean for you? And why?

How does the knowledge of the coming of the Lord—and His judgment—encourage you to witness?

4. What is at least one truth or response you need to take away from Luke 12? Write it here, and record it in Lesson 25.

Living with Passion and Purpose

As we think now about living with passion and purpose, we see, once again, that Jesus remained passionate about His message, especially as He moved toward the cross. Sadly, His sermon on hypocrisy further inflamed the hatred of the religious leaders toward Him. Yet His message is loud and clear: All must get right with God! Judgment is coming!

Dear friend, are you facing opposition at home? At work? From extended family members? Jesus warned that division would come. Ask God to help you stand firm in faith. And what about the coming judgment? Ask God to give you love and boldness to speak of Jesus' return, even to those who are hostile toward you and the gospel message. Don't give up on others. Jesus didn't.

Focusing on the Kingdom

Luke 13

*I*n our household, both Jim and I make to-do lists every morning, seven days a week, no matter where we are. From the minute we complete our lists, we depend on our written priorities to guide us as we make decisions about how to use our time and energy during the day. The lists help us to focus our momentum and our decision making.

It's the same way when it comes to God's plan for our lives, only His is a "life list," not a daily list. Are you conscious of your purpose in life, and are you expressing that purpose in your decision-making? How are you practically living out God's plan and purpose each day? Stand by and watch the Master life manager as He focuses—with passion and purpose—on His divine to-do list, which in Luke 13 is proclaiming the kingdom of God. As one has written regarding His focus, "What determination was Christ's to fulfil a God-given task!"[5]

God's Message...

1. Read Luke 13:1-9. Describe the scene here.

   What was the assumption of the people?

   How did Jesus correct their assumption?

   What was Jesus' message in His "Parable of the Fig Tree"?

2. Read Luke 13:10-17. Israel's leaders had long been critical of Jesus regarding the Sabbath day. What occurred here, and what was the problem? (Incidentally, this is the last mention in Luke that Jesus taught in a synagogue.)

   How did Jesus address the leaders, and how did He handle their criticism?

3. Read Luke 13:18-21. After being interrupted, Jesus continued on. What did He teach concerning the kingdom of God?

How do Matthew 13:31-33 and Mark 4:30-32 help explain Jesus' meaning?

4. Read Luke 13:22-30. What does Luke again remind his readers of in verse 22?

Jesus had already expanded and intensified His ministry. Now He focused it. Upon what (verse 22)?

What happens to those who reject the Master (verse 27)?

5. Read Luke 13:31-35. What warning was given to Jesus?

How did Jesus respond?

What was His attitude toward Jerusalem and the nation of Israel?

...and Your Heart's Response

1. How does Jesus' message to the nation of Israel in Luke 13:1-9 apply to your life?

What immediate changes should you make in your thinking?

2. In light of "The Parable of the Mustard Seed" and "The Parable of the Leaven," what are your responsibilities in relation to the kingdom of God?

3. What is more important than knowing how many will be saved (verses 23-24)?

How did Jesus describe the way into the kingdom (verse 24)?

Can you think of erroneous assumptions people today make about their merits for entering into the kingdom of God?

What is it that merits your entrance into the kingdom?

4. Read again Jesus' lament over Jerusalem and Israel's rejection in verses 34-35. What qualities in the Savior are revealed by His attitude?

5. What is at least one truth or response you need to take away from Luke 13? Write it here, and record it in Lesson 25.

Living with Passion and Purpose

As I already said, Jesus was the Master manager! We've just seen Him continue to head toward Jerusalem, all the while impressing upon His listeners the need for repentance if they would enter into the kingdom of God. You see, the kingdom had come, whether the people realized it or not (Luke 11:20). Therefore Jesus focused on teaching the people, using a variety of parables to describe what the kingdom of God is like.

Lesson 14

Growing in Humility

Luke 14

Many rely on "Miss Manners" or longtime etiquette expert Amy Vanderbilt for guidelines for proper conduct and behavior at a dinner party. But Jesus has His own divine set of guidelines for us. He shows us in Luke 14 what is far more significant than a familiarity with each eating utensil and knowing when to use it during the course of a meal, or knowing how to make introductions and carry on sparkling, entertaining conversation. Read on and pay attention as Jesus shows us that people are more important than securing a position in society or following a set of rules, and that humility is more important than who you sit next to at the next big dinner party.

God's Message...

1. Read Luke 14:1-24. As you consider verses 1-6, describe when and where this scene takes place.

   What were the Pharisees' motives?

   What happened during this dinner?

   What question did Jesus ask?

   When no one dared to answer, how did Jesus answer His own question:

   Physically—

   Verbally—

2. Look again at verses 7-14. What did Jesus observe about those attending the dinner?

   What message did Jesus send through "The Parable of the Ambitious Guest"?

   How did Jesus exhort His host in verses 12-13, and what character qualities would such action require or reveal?

3. Look again at verses 15-24. Many in Israel believed that only Jews would be invited to the heavenly feast. How did Jesus refute this belief in His "Parable of the Great Supper"?

4. Read Luke 14:25-35. What happened when Jesus left the dinner in verse 25, and how did Jesus take advantage of the situation?

What requirements did Jesus give concerning being His disciple in:

Verse 26—

Verse 27—

Verses 28-33—

How did Jesus end His teaching on discipleship in verses 34-35?

...and Your Heart's Response

1. According to Jesus, what is acceptable conduct on any day of worship (Luke 14:1-5)?

Who needs your ministry at church this week?

2. In verses 8-14, Jesus chastised and instructed those guests at the dinner who ambitiously sought the best seats. What did Paul have to say along this line in Philippians 2:3-4?

When you attend a dinner, what does Jesus say you should remember to do?

When you host a dinner, what does Jesus say you should remember to do?

3. Briefly categorize the excuses given for not attending the great supper in Luke 14:16-24.

How can property, possessions, and people keep us from following after the things of God?

When Christ has first place in your heart, how is your attitude toward property, possessions, and people changed?

4. Think again about Jesus' message in verses 26-33. What does following Jesus and "cross bearing" imply?

How do verses 34-35 instruct you regarding your influence upon others as a Christian?

How can the failure of a believer to follow Christ as a disciple cause him or her to live a meaningless life with little passion and purpose?

5. What is at least one truth or response you need to take away from Luke 14? Write it here, and record it in Lesson 25.

Living with Passion and Purpose

This Bible study falls under the umbrella of helping you and me become "A Woman After God's Own Heart." As we pause here to evaluate our hearts and ou level of humility, how would you describe your level of discipleship? Is your interest in living for Jesus wholehearted or only running at half-a-heart? The psalmist declared, "My soul follows close behind You" (Psalm 63:8). Are you following "hard" after God (KJV), or are you more of a casual follower who makes some effort if it's convenient and the cost isn't too great?

My friend, God does not desire to be on the trivial end of your list of priorities. Maybe the time has come to make some harder choices and increase the level of your commitment to God and your passion for Christ. Discipleship is costly. What price are you willing to pay? Jesus' disciples "were permitted to retain no privileges and make no demands. They were to safeguard no cherished sins; treasure no earthly possessions; and cling to no secret self-indulgences. Their commitment to Him must be without reservation."[6] They were to "forsake all" (Luke 14:33).

Lesson 15

Discovering the
Heart of God

Luke 15

The question is often asked (and I've already asked it myself as I've been making my way through the many parables in Luke): Why did Jesus use so many parables in His teaching? And...what is a parable, anyway? To answer, a parable is an illustration from everyday life that is "placed alongside" (that's the literal meaning of the word *parable*) to help explain a teaching. Jesus was a master teacher, and He used parables to help His listeners—and us—understand truths.

Once again, in this chapter, Jesus was facing opposition from the religious leaders. This time they were again upset about Jesus' association with "sinners," and Jesus answered the leaders through three parables describing the joy of God at the repentance of even one sinner. For you and me today, these parables are both an invitation to rejoice with God at

85

the forgiveness of one lone sinner as well as a reminder for us to enter into the search for the lost.

God's Message...

1. Read Luke 15:1-2. Describe the scene. Who was present, what happened, and what was the accusation?

2. Read Luke 15:3-7. How did Jesus respond to the criticism?

   Briefly summarize the message of Jesus' "Parable of the Lost Sheep," the first of three parables designed to reveal the true attitude of God toward those who are lost.

   What was the shepherd's attitude when he found the lost sheep, and how did he express it?

   What point did Jesus make to His listeners?

3. Read Luke 15:8-10. Briefly summarize the message of Jesus' "Parable of the Lost Coin."

   What was the woman's attitude when she found the lost coin, and how did she express it?

What point did Jesus make to His listeners?

4. Read Luke 15:11-32. Briefly summarize the message of Jesus' "Parable of the Lost Son."

What was the prodigal son's attitude when he:

Left home—

Returned home—

What was the father's attitude when his lost son returned home, and how did he express it?

What was the older son's attitude when he heard of his brother's return?

5. What does each parable in Luke 15 emphasize about searching?

—

—

—

...and Your Heart's Response

1. Regarding "The Parable of the Lost Sheep," how was compassion toward and the importance of one lost sheep demonstrated?

   What is God's message here to your heart concerning one lost soul?

2. Regarding "The Parable of the Lost Coin," how was the value and importance of one lost coin demonstrated?

   What is God's message here to your heart concerning one lost soul?

3. Regarding "The Parable of the Lost Son," list several lessons you learn from:

   The prodigal son—

   The older son—

   The father—

   What do you think the Pharisees were meant to learn from Luke 15:25-32?

4. Based on the parables in Luke 15, what several things have you learned about the heart of your heavenly Father?

5. What is at least one truth or response you need to take away from Luke 15? Write it here, and record it in Lesson 25.

Living with Passion and Purpose

This chapter has been called "an inspired revelation of the heart of God."[7] His is a heart of love and persistence when it comes to sinners. Would this describe your heart? Your activities toward those who do not know the Savior? Is there a neighbor, a fellow soccer mom, or someone at work you can befriend so they can hear about the heart of God? Join God in His search for the lost by telling your family, friends, workmates—even strangers—about Jesus. Pray for your very own opportunity to rejoice over their salvation!

Lesson 16

Making the Most of Opportunity

hether you and I acknowledge it or not, nothing that is ours is truly ours, whether it is our homes, our finances, our husbands, our children, or our health...and ultimately our lives. All of life is a stewardship, and you and I are asked by God to make the most of each opportunity. A steward is one who is accountable to another. In our case, we answer to God for all He entrusts us with. In this chapter we'll hear Jesus again use parables to show us a steward who wasted his master's goods and, worse yet, a man who wasted his life. Keep in mind, as you read, these words from the apostle Paul: "Moreover it is required in stewards that one be found faithful" (1 Corinthians 4:2).

God's Message...

1. Read Luke 16:1-13. Jesus continues to teach the tax collectors, sinners, Pharisees, and His disciples (see 15:1-2). First He tells "The Parable of the Unjust Servant." Briefly note the highlights of the scene in 16:1-2.

   What did the unjust steward do in verses 2-7?

   How did the steward's master respond? Why?

2. After telling this story, to what subject did Jesus turn His attention in Luke 16:9-13? (As you read, keep in mind that the word "mammon" means money and material riches.)

   List Jesus' teachings here regarding faithfulness.

   Money is a part of everyday life, but Jesus taught that spiritual life and matters are far more important. What was His final message in verse 13?

3. Read Luke 16:14-18. How did the Pharisees respond to the message of Jesus' parable?

How did Jesus illustrate that merely keeping the law was not enough, and what did He say is more important (verse 15)?

4. As you read Luke 16:18, remember that Jesus was frequently accused of violating God's law. How did Jesus let the religious leaders know that the unfailing law of God was still in effect (verse 17)?

5. Read "The Parable of the Rich Man and Lazarus" in Luke 16:19-31. Describe:

The rich man—

Lazarus—

What common event did the two men share, and how did it affect:

The rich man—

Lazarus—

What made the difference in their eternal outcomes?

What was Jesus' message to those listening regarding:

Wealth—

Poverty—

Listening to the Word of God—

...and Your Heart's Response

1. As most scholars note, the point of Jesus' parable about the unjust steward is not that dishonesty is commendable, but that the steward's prudent provision for the future was commendable. How can your money be used to provide "spiritual capital" for the future, according to:

   Matthew 6:19-21—

   1 Corinthians 9:6-8—

   1 Timothy 6:17-19—

2. What do these verses teach about our inability to serve both God and the world, which includes money?

   James 4:4—

1 John 2:15-16—

3. Write brief statements about what God is teaching you in Luke 16 in regard to:

Stewardship—

Faithfulness—

Money—

Serving God—

The Word of God—

4. What is at least one truth or response you need to take away from Luke 16? Write it here, and record it in Lesson 25.

Living with Passion and Purpose

Everyone wonders about life after death. Well, good news! You are blessed to be studying the Gospel of Luke because only Luke recorded Jesus' parable that gives us a glimpse of life beyond this earth. What we have learned here from the lips of Jesus is sobering. Through His "Parable of the Rich Man and Lazarus" we witnessed a poverty-ridden beggar's dying and entering a life of pleasure after an earthly existence of torment. We also read about the death of a rich man who lived his days on earth in splendor...and woke up to eternal torment and agony. What made the difference? Poor Lazarus had made the most of his spiritual opportunities on earth, while the rich man had lived for money only.

My friend, clearly the ultimate stewardship required is that of your life. How can you be a better steward of your days on earth?

Lesson 17

Dealing with Life Issues

Luke 17

For many years our family lived in sunny Southern California. It definitely was not a problem to get used to the incredibly beautiful weather. But one thing that was hard to adjust to was the cement block walls between every home in our neighborhood. Those walls made it difficult to have a relationship with neighbors. And, if we are not careful, we can build walls around our hearts and lives that make it difficult to respond in the right way—God's way—to the people and life issues that come our way.

Open your heart—and your ears—and hear Jesus' words as He continues to make His way to Jerusalem, all the while teaching. He wants us to understand how to forgive others, accept our positions in life, and give thanks, all the while watching for Him to come again.

God's Message...

1. Read Luke 17:1-6. To whom did Jesus turn His attention, and what was His message concerning forgiveness?

   How did those present respond?

   What answer did Jesus give to them?

2. Read Luke 17:7-10. What "absurd" illustration did Jesus use to define service?

   What attitude did Jesus say should be at the heart of every servant?

3. Read Luke 17:11-19. Again, where was Jesus' focus (verse 11)?

   What happened as Jesus traveled (verses 12-13)?

   How did Jesus reply to the request?

   What happened next (verses 15-16)?

   What was Jesus' response?

4. Read Luke 17:20-37. Here, Jesus began instruction concerning His second coming. This instruction continues on until Luke 18:8. What launched His teaching on this subject (Luke 17:20)?

What was Jesus' "short answer" as to where one should look for the kingdom of God (verse 21)?

Briefly, what did Jesus say to His disciples about:

Looking for the kingdom of God (verses 22-24)—

What had to occur before the kingdom of God arrived (verse 25)—

The manner in which the kingdom of God would arrive (verses 26-30)—

How to respond to the coming of the kingdom of God (verses 31-37)—

...and Your Heart's Response

1. Outline Jesus' teaching on forgiveness as presented in Luke 17:3-4.

How have you shown forgiveness recently?

2. What are some common rewards people expect for their labors and service?

Why did Jesus say this is a wrong attitude?

Think about your service to God and others. Do any adjustments need to be made in your expectations or motives?

3. What did Mary say about God's work in her life in Luke 1:49?

What has God done for you, and are you faithful to express your thankfulness? List several ways you can express your gratitude.

4. According to 1 Peter 1:13, how should you live as you wait for Jesus to return?

5. What is at least one truth or response you need to take away from Luke 17? Write it here, and record it in Lesson 25.

Living with Passion and Purpose

In the book of Luke, we see Jesus' purpose and passion mounting minute by minute as He marched toward Jerusalem and the "life issue"—the cross—that awaited Him there. What life issues are you dealing with at this moment? In light of Jesus' second coming, don't put off forgiveness, faithfulness, and thankfulness. Whatever your challenges are, you have God's grace available to you to help you do the right thing, to deal with it His way. As one scholar exhorts us, "Life is short. Therefore opportunities to make our lives 'shine for Jesus' should be grasped."[8]

Lesson 18

Surrendering Soul and Substance

Luke 18

Whenever I work on a project or make a commitment to do something, one of two things usually happens. Either I get really excited and my passion becomes even more extreme, or I begin to lose interest and my energy and focus dissolve into impatience and halfheartedness.

Praise God for the perfect Son of Man! Jesus' commitment to the cross was a continuously burning passion, and His interest, energy, and focus never waned for a second. And, along the way, He was equally intent on preparing His disciples for His death and their ministry afterward. How did Jesus go about preparing 12 imperfect men? He did it by instructing them to be persistent in prayer, to grow in humility, and to surrender soul and substance to follow Him.

God's Message...

1. Read Luke 18:1-8. Here Jesus continued the discussion begun in Luke 17 concerning the kingdom of God. He assured His disciples that, at the coming of the Son of Man, life would be hard for God's people (Luke 18:7-8). What did Jesus want them to do and not do at that time (verse 1)?

   Describe the judge and his actions in Jesus' "Parable of the Woman and the Judge."

   Describe the woman and her actions in this same parable.

   How did Jesus use this parable to illustrate the importance of persistence in prayer?

2. Read "The Parable of the Pharisee and the Tax Collector" in Luke 18:9-14. To whom was this parable directed (verse 9)?

   Briefly describe the prayers of the two men:

   The Pharisee—

   The tax collector—

What was Jesus' commentary on the two men's prayers?

What principle did Jesus state in verse 14?

3. Read Luke 18:15-30. Here we see the people around Jesus responding to Him in a variety of ways. From verses 15-17, describe the scene and include information regarding:

The parents—

The disciples—

Jesus' actions and attitude—

Jesus' words—

From verses 18-27, describe the encounter and include information regarding:

The rich young ruler's question—

Jesus' answer—

The rich young ruler's reply—

Jesus' additional instructions—

The rich young ruler's response—

Jesus' principle—

The people's response—

In your own words, restate the principle Jesus uttered in verses 29-30.

4. Read Luke 18:31-43. Where was Jesus headed, and of what does He again remind His disciples in verses 31-34?

Describe what happened along the way and the request made to Jesus in verse 41.

Contrast the people's response to the man in need with Jesus' response.

...and Your Heart's Response

1. Think back through this lesson on Luke 18. What is taught here regarding:

   Trials—

   Prayer—

   Riches—

   Eternal life—

   Ministering to those in need—

2. Jesus' theme for much of Luke 18 is discipleship, what it means to follow Him. Is there anything keeping you back from a complete surrender to following Christ? As you pray about what it means to follow Him, determine what you will do to be a more committed disciple.

3. What is at least one truth or response you need to take away from Luke 18? Write it here, and record it in Lesson 25.

Living with Passion and Purpose

These poignant words teach us much about how Jesus lived with passion and purpose: "With the shadow of the cross darkening the path of the Lord Jesus, we find Him solemnly warning His disciples of coming trials. They must expect to share His bitter cup. On the way to die, He yet went on with His task. The call of human need never went unheeded."[9] May we follow in His steps!

Lesson 19

Preparing for King and Kingdom

Luke 19

*I*n Oklahoma, where I grew up, Palm Sunday was significant for two reasons. First of all, I knew when this special Sunday rolled around that winter was over...and spring was here to stay. But more importantly, this was the day we remembered Jesus' entry into Jerusalem. In my little church, the people present received small palm branches or fronds when they entered the church building. There were special songs and choral arrangements and a sermon describing Jesus' road to the cross that following Friday, not to mention special crafts around my little Sunday-school table.

As we now read Luke 19 and the details of that first Palm Sunday, take a few minutes to recall your own special memories of Palm Sundays past.

God's Message...

1. Read Luke 19:1-10. Who was Zacchaeus, and what actions did he take that expressed a sincere heart and an earnest attitude toward Jesus?

   What were the results of Zacchaeus's desire and efforts?

2. Read Luke 19:11-27, Jesus' "Parable of the Ten Minas." How did Jesus show His followers what their behavior should be while waiting for the kingdom of God to arrive?

   The master in the parable gave each man the same opportunity, the same amount of money. Briefly describe the actions and attitudes of:

   The first man—

   The second man—

   The third man—

   How did the master deal with each man?

What principle is given in verse 26?

3. Read Luke 19:28-40. Again, where was Jesus headed?

Sketch out the order of events in verses 28-37.

What confrontation occurred in verse 38, and how did Jesus answer?

4. Read Luke 19:41-44. At last, Jesus reached Jerusalem! What effect did it have upon Him? And why?

5. Read Luke 19:45-48. What was Jesus' first act when He arrived in Jerusalem? Why?

From that point on, how did Jesus spend His time?

How did the religious leaders and rulers spend their time?

...and Your Heart's Response

1. As a result of his encounter with Jesus, Zacchaeus's life was changed. Share several ways your life has changed,

or several changes you have made, as a result of knowing Jesus.

2. According to Luke 19:11-27, what behavior should we exhibit while we wait for the kingdom of God to arrive?

Your concept of God is reflected in your obedience and service. How are you doing at living out the attitudes and character demonstrated by the good servants in "The Parable of the Ten Minas"?

3. How does Jesus' sorrow in verses 41-44 over the souls of those who did not receive Him instruct your heart for the lost and for those who reject Christ?

4. Like Jesus in verses 45-48, what are you doing to teach others about Christ as the day of His return approaches?

5. What is at least one truth or response you need to take away from Luke 19? Write it here, and record it in Lesson 25.

Living with Passion and Purpose

We are hushed as we realize that the final week of Jesus' life on earth has arrived. The Gospel of Luke is coming to a dramatic end. As we've studied our way through Luke, we have seen our Lord steadfastly preparing for this specific time. Even at the tender age of 12, He knew His purpose (Luke 2:49). And now, three short years after He began His ministry at the age of 30, Jesus had inflamed a nation with His passion. He had faithfully taught His disciples. He had tirelessly addressed the multitudes. He had miraculously healed individuals. And He had consistently angered the Jewish religious leaders.

Yet, as Jesus entered Jerusalem, He wept, for He knew the people were not looking for a spiritual Savior. They were looking for a conquering hero who would return their nation to past glories. Sadly, and with tears, He predicted the destruction of Jerusalem, which would occur 40 years later—a divine judgment from God for the people's failure to recognize and embrace their Messiah when He visited them.[10]

Have you recognized and embraced Christ as the Messiah sent from God? If not, make it a priority to prepare yourself for the King and His kingdom. If so, rejoice. Praise God for His mercy and grace. And be sure to share the gospel with others, that they might be saved.

Lesson 20

Questioning Jesus' Authority

Luke 20

ave you heard a saying that says, in essence, When Plan A doesn't work, switch to Plan B? Well, in Luke 20, we witness the religious leaders doing just that. Instead of continuing to question Jesus' authority by making outright accusations and to verbalize their criticism and judgment, they switched their tactics and began to pose clever questions to Him when He was in public. These queries were designed to trick or trap Jesus with His own words.

Be on your toes as we head into this stirring chapter as the all-powerful Christ not only headed for the cross, but ran head-on into the leaders of "the people [who] sought to destroy Him" (Luke 19:47), all the while continuing to faithfully teach His disciples...and us.

God's Message...

1. Read Luke 20:1-8. Who confronted Jesus, and what was the key issue (verse 2)?

   How did Jesus answer in verse 3?

   How did this situation end (verses 5-8)?

2. Read Luke 20:9-19. Continuing on with the issue raised by the Jewish leaders, Jesus told "The Parable of the Vineyard Owner" to illustrate the true spiritual situation in Israel. Briefly retell the parable in a few sentences.

   Contrast how the servants in the parable were treated with how the beloved son was treated.

   How did the Jewish leaders understand Jesus' message (verse 19)?

3. Read Luke 20:20-26. What was the next question designed to snare Jesus?

   How did Jesus answer that question?

4. Read Luke 20:27-40. What was the next issue the religious leaders brought up to Jesus (see verses 27 and 33)?

Briefly list what Jesus revealed about the nature of life after death in verses 34-36.

These Jews did not believe in life after death because, for one reason, it was not taught in the Pentateuch, the five books of the Bible written by Moses. Yet how did Jesus answer their objections in verses 37-38?

5. Read Luke 20:41-47. How did Jesus address the fact of His humanity and deity, that He was both God and man?

What was Jesus' warning to His disciples concerning the Jewish leaders?

...and Your Heart's Response

1. What do you learn about Jesus' wisdom, authority, and knowledge of men's hearts in Luke 20:1-8?

2. How does Jesus' answer to His enemies in verse 25 apply to you today?

What does Romans 13:1-7 say, reiterating Jesus' teaching?

How does Jesus' teaching affect your view of paying taxes?

3. Read John 11:25-26. What do these verses tell you about the resurrection, and how do they comfort you?

4. What did you learn from Jesus' description of your eternal state in Luke 20:34-36? Share it here.

5. Look again at the practices of the Jewish leaders in verses 46-47. Do you see any such practices or attitudes in yourself? Recall now some of Jesus' teachings thus far in the Gospel of Luke about better practices and attitudes.

6. What is at least one truth or response you need to take away from Luke 20? Write it here, and record it in Lesson 25.

Living with Passion and Purpose

As we are continually witnessing, the Jews of Jesus' day rejected Him who "became the chief cornerstone" (Luke 20:17). To them, He was a stumbling stone. Yet to us who believe in Him, He is the foundation stone, the cornerstone on whom the church is built (1 Corinthians 1:23).

Jesus embraced every part of His life with passion and purpose. Whether it was tending to someone unfortunate and in need or teaching His disciples what they needed to know, whether it was striding toward His appointment with the cross or doing battle with His enemies, everything had a purpose and was handled with a passionate zeal for doing the Father's will. Indeed, as the Scriptures report, "He has done all things well" (Mark 7:37).

May this be true of you and me. May we sense God's purpose in all that touches us. And may we live out every encounter and challenge with a passionate love for God and desire for bringing Him honor and glory.

Looking to the Future

Luke 21

ost employers allow for an "off day," an occasional goof, or a lapse in good judgment. But for a prophet, there could be no off days. To be a true prophet required being on target 100 percent of the time. Obviously, because Jesus was God and knew the end from the beginning, His predictions were always completely accurate.

In Luke 21 Jesus reveals to all the end-times for His people. He tells them, and us, how to look to the future and how to live through those difficult times. He also shows us how He Himself chose to spend His final days and hours on earth as He looked to His future. Prepare yourself for information that is both sobering and instructive.

God's Message...

1. Read Luke 21:1-4. After a tumultuous time of opposition
   and confrontation, Jesus had a moment to sit quietly.
   What did He observe in the temple?

   Contrast the giving of the wealthy versus that of the
   widow.

   What conclusion did Jesus draw from His observations?

2. Read Luke 21:5-38. Here we read Luke's account of Jesus'
   message delivered to His disciples in answer to their concern regarding the coming judgment and other future
   events. How did they broach their concern in verses 5-7,
   and what two basic questions did they ask?

   In verses 8-19, Jesus pictured the sufferings of His disciples
   during the time between His ascension into heaven and
   the overthrow of Jerusalem. List several of Jesus' warn-
   ings in verses 8-11.

List several ways Jesus' followers would suffer, according to verses 12-19.

List several positive assurances Jesus gave His followers in verses 12-19.

Look again through the Savior's instruction. What urgent words of exhortation did He use to impress upon His listeners and followers the importance of His message (see verses 8 and 14)?

3. Read Luke 21:20-24. What instruction did Jesus give to those who would be present at the fall of Jerusalem?

4. Read Luke 21:25-38. Here Jesus continued His teaching regarding the prophecy of Jerusalem's destruction. What was Jesus' final warning to His hearers (verses 34-36)?

How did Jesus choose to spend His last days on earth (verses 37-38)?

...and Your Heart's Response

1. As you think about the poor woman's sacrifice in Luke 21:1-4, examine your own giving:

   Your motives for giving—

   Your methods for giving—

   The amount of your giving—

   The heart of your giving—

   What additional instruction does 2 Corinthians 9:6-7 have regarding your giving?

2. After looking closely at Luke 21:5-19, what quality do you think is most key to enduring the future events Jesus spoke of, and how are you displaying this quality in your daily life?

3. As you read again Jesus' instructions and example in verses 34-38 about how to live each day, what changes do you need to make in your:

Lifestyle—

Focus—

Passion—

4. What is at least one truth or response you need to take away from Luke 21? Write it here, and record it in Lesson 25.

Living with Passion and Purpose

Jesus spoke of His people as "shining as lights" (see Matthew 5:14-16). As the darkness of our times grows thicker and the time of Jesus' brilliant reappearing draws closer, we ought to live each of our remaining days with greater purpose, with a fiery urgency, and with a passion for the souls of those who do not know our Savior.

Whom do you know who needs to hear about the Savior today? How can you contribute financially today to further the message of the gospel? And how can you choose to spend your time so that the lives of others are enriched?

Lesson 22

Doing God's Will

Luke 22

Do you ever go through a day when everything seems escalated, when event piles upon event, when you must move from one happening to the next...and in rapid order? Luke chapter 22 shows us Jesus' life moving toward the culmination and completion of His purpose. In this chapter we witness Jesus carefully planning and preparing for His final hours with His loved ones. Then we see Him in an extended prayer time with His heavenly Father as He prepared for the end of His time on earth. And finally Jesus was not only arrested by His enemies, but betrayed by His friends. What a day!

But...what a Savior!

God's Message...

1. Read Luke 22:1-6. As Jesus began to teach all day long (see Luke 21:37-38), what did the religious leaders do?

   How were the Jewish leaders aided by one of Jesus' very own disciples?

2. Read Luke 22:7-20. With whom did Jesus spend His last Passover?

   What indicates that Jesus carefully planned for this Passover time?

   What information did Jesus share at dinner in verse 15?

3. Read Luke 22:21-38. What new subject did Jesus bring up in verses 21-22?

   How did the disciples react in:

   Verse 23—

   Verse 24—

What lesson did Jesus have for them in verses 25-27?

What special words did Jesus have for Peter in verses 31-34?

What further instruction did Jesus give to His disciples in verses 35-38?

4. Read Luke 22:39-46. Briefly describe:

Jesus' instructions to His disciples—

Jesus' condition—

Jesus' prayers—

Jesus' companions—

5. Read Luke 22:47-71. In a very few words, summarize these events:

Jesus' encounter with Judas and the priests—

The injury and healing of the servant of the high priest—

The arrest of Jesus in Gethsemane—

Peter's denial—

Jesus' treatment by the soldiers—

Jesus' trial before the Jewish leaders—

...and Your Heart's Response

1. What do you learn in this chapter about:

   True greatness—

   Jesus' power over Satan—

   Prayer—

   Handling difficult times—

2. What is at least one truth or response you need to take away from Luke 22? Write it here, and record it in Lesson 25.

Living with Passion and Purpose

This chapter is hard to read! It hurts us to see our Savior in pain of both soul and body. Yet, as with every action and word thus far, He shows us a picture of faithful obedience and sincere love for the Father and how each is lived out. In Him we learn how to do God's will. We witness in Him the power that purpose provides for helping one face difficult times and seeing one through pain. We eavesdrop on His agonizing times in passionate prayer, ending with His commitment to do God's will—"Not My will, but Yours, be done" (verse 42).

Dear one, as incredible as it seems, by God's grace we, too, can endure difficult times. We, too, can do God's will. We, through prayer, can "come boldly to the throne of grace that we may obtain mercy and find grace to help in time of need" (Hebrews 4:16). We have God's promise that His "grace is sufficient" for us and His "strength is made perfect" in our weakness (2 Corinthians 12:9). We also have God's statement of fact, that we have already been given "all things that pertain to life and godliness" (2 Peter 1:3)—everything we need to live lives of passion and purpose. And, blessing upon blessing, our Lord left us "an example, that [we] should follow His steps" (1 Peter 2:21). May we ever carry His perfect example in our minds and hearts as we seek to do God's will.

Lesson 23

Fulfilling God's Purpose

Luke 23

*I*n chapter 23 of Luke, we step into the darkest hour of history on earth, the time of the crucifixion of Jesus, the Son of God and the Son of Man. And how did our Jesus face death, deal with pain, and endure false accusations, unjust punishment, and a railing mob? As always, we learn volumes from His perfect conduct, gracious heart, and resolute purpose. As you read on, take note of His forgiving spirit, His habit of prayer, His continued ministry to others to His last breath, and His never-failing trust in the Father.

God's Message...

1. Read Luke 23:1-25. In Luke 22, Jesus was tried before the

Jewish leaders. Before whom was Jesus taken for trial in Luke 23:1-5, and what were the accusations against Him?

Before whom was He next tried in verses 6-12? How was He treated, and why?

What was determined about Jesus in verses 13-15 and 22?

What did the people demand in verses 16-25?

2. Read Luke 23:26-31. As we have witnessed, by this time Jesus had been struck, beaten, and scourged (a practice that could in itself kill a person). What became necessary in order for Jesus to continue on toward His crucifixion, and who was the one to assist (verse 26)?

What warning did Jesus give to the mourning women in verses 27-31?

3. Read Luke 23:32-49. What name was given to the place where Jesus was crucified, and who was crucified along with Him (verses 32-33)?

What were Jesus' first words after being nailed to the cross (verse 34)?

How was Jesus treated at this time (verses 35-38)?

Describe the interchange between Jesus and the two criminals:

Criminal #1—

Criminal #2—

What glorious assurance did Jesus give the second thief, and what does it teach us about the requirements for heaven?

As you review verses 44-49, describe the miracle that occurred.

What variety of reactions do you see in:

The centurion—

The people—

Jesus' friends and the women—

4. Read Luke 23:50-56. Whom do we meet in verses 50-53? Describe him and what he did.

Who else cared for Jesus, and how (verses 55-56)?

...and Your Heart's Response

1. We stand amazed at Jesus' conduct under fire at trial, during physical affliction, and in excruciating pain. What additional insights into His behavior do we gain in:

   Philippians 2:5-8—

   1 Peter 2:19-23—

2. Read Psalm 22 and list some of the information given in this prophetic psalm about the suffering Savior that is fulfilled in Luke 23.

3. In Luke 23, what impresses you most about:

   Jesus' conduct during His trials—

   Jesus' interaction with others—

   Jesus' sense of purpose—

Jesus' prayer life—

Those who assisted Jesus—

4. What is at least one truth or response you need to take away from Luke 23? Write it here, and record it in Lesson 25.

Living with Passion and Purpose

As one has noted, "the Lord Jesus was made to stand before Pilate and Herod. But *He* was not on trial. The *rulers* were, and their contact with Him revealed what they really were."[11] What is most important as you and I finish this chapter and contemplate its content is that we review what our contact with Jesus' life and death reveals about our relationship with Jesus Christ, Son of Man and Son of God.

Is Jesus the passion and purpose of your life? Is He your Savior? Have you put your trust in Him? And do you have the assurance of eternal life?

Lesson 24

Responding to the Resurrection

Luke 24

The glory of Easter is the resurrection of Jesus Christ. Yes, Jesus suffered...horribly. And yes, He died a terrible death. But, miracle of miracles, Jesus rose physically from death (Romans 1:4). Perhaps you can recall the thrill of singing on Easter Sunday the time-honored words, "up from the grave He arose," from the hymn "Christ Arose."[12] There's no way to remain sitting in your seat while singing this triumphant song!

Chapter 23 of Luke closed on a dark and dreary note—with the death of Jesus. Death is where the biographies of all men end. But not so with Jesus. Stand by for a victorious event! Watch for an "opened grave, opened eyes, opened Scriptures, opened understandings, and opened heaven"[13]!

God's Message...

1. Read Luke 24:1-12. Who were the first followers to discover the empty tomb of the resurrected Savior? Briefly describe what happened in verses 1-7 at the tomb and the conversation that occurred.

   What happened next (verses 8-10), and what was the response of Jesus' disciples (verse 11)?

   What did Peter do and discover in verse 12?

2. Read Luke 24:13-35. What was occurring in verses 13-16?

   As Jesus talked with the two men, what did they report to Him (verses 17-24)?

   How did Jesus answer them in their dismay (verses 25-27)?

   What purpose was involved in Jesus' suffering, according to verse 26?

As Jesus and His disciples sat at dinner, what happened, and what was the disciples' response in:

Verses 28-32—

Verses 33-35—

3. Read Luke 24:36-48. How did the disciples respond when Jesus appeared to them?

List the ways Jesus sought to calm and assure His disciples as He revealed Himself to them in His glory (verses 36-43).

What did Jesus finally do for His baffled disciples (verses 44-48)?

4. Read Luke 24:49-53. What was Jesus' final promise (see also John 14:26 and Acts 1:8) and instruction to His disciples in verse 49?

What was Jesus' final act, and what happened at that time (verses 50-51)?

How did the disciples respond (verses 52-53)?

...and Your Heart's Response

1. What fact was reported in the following instances:

   The angels to the women at the tomb (Luke 24:6)—

   The women to the disciples (verse 10)—

   The two Emmaus travelers to the disciples (verse 34)—

   Jesus to the disciples (verse 46)—

2. Look again at verse 47. This mission mandate was Christ's final instruction to His followers before ascending into heaven. How important should it be to you?

3. Note again the condition of the two disciples on the road to Emmaus (verse 17) and those who gathered for dinner (verses 37-38). Contrast these conditions of the heart with those experienced after Jesus "expounded to them in all the Scriptures the things concerning Himself" (verse 27) and that which was "written in the Law of Moses and the Prophets and the Psalms" (verse 44) concerning Messiah. How does the faithful study of the Bible, the Word of God, help us in our understanding and increase our joy?

4. How has the study of the Gospel of Luke helped you with your:

Understanding of Jesus, the Son of Man—

Understanding of Jesus' resurrection—

Understanding of Jesus' passion—

Understanding of Jesus' purpose—

Understanding of your passion—

Understanding of your purpose—

5. What is at least one truth or response you need to take away from Luke 24? Write it here, and record it in Lesson 25.

6. What would you next like to study and learn more about from the Bible, and what is your plan for following through on your desire?

Living with Passion and Purpose

What an incredible experience Jesus' faithful followers had when He rose from the dead and appeared to them once again before He ascended into heaven! Imagine... walking and talking with the risen Lord! Imagine...hearing the Scriptures explained out of His omniscience and from His very own lips! Imagine...sitting to dine with the glorious risen Christ! Imagine...beholding the Son of Man being carried up into heaven! Indeed, Jesus' disciples were blessed.

However, as Jesus told Thomas, "Because you have seen Me, you have believed. Blessed are those who have not seen and yet have believed" (John 20:29). You and I fall into this latter category, those who have *not* seen. So the question to you now is, do you believe?

Every person on earth must respond to the truth about Jesus Christ, to the facts of His birth, death, burial, and resurrection. As you end this study on the life of Christ, please do these three things:

- First, if you are a believer in Jesus Christ, thank God profusely that He has, as it were, opened your understanding that you might comprehend who Jesus Christ is.

- Second, as a believer in Christ, go forward from this moment on and do as Jesus told His disciples—preach to others that "it was necessary for the Christ to suffer and to rise from the dead the third day, and that repentance and remission of sins should be preached in His name to all nations" (Luke 24:46-47).

- And third, if you are unsure of your salvation through Jesus Christ, pray. Pray for God to graciously impress upon your heart the truths about Jesus Christ, to enable you to believe in Jesus and to receive Him as your Savior (see John 1:12). Step One for living your life with passion and purpose is to know the Savior.

Lesson 25

Learning to Live with Passion and Purpose

Take-Away Truths

*O*ver the years I have kept a journal of important dates, events, and growth in my life. No price can be put on such a record! I carry it with me at all times and review it regularly. And each time I open it, I am encouraged, stimulated, taught again, refreshed, and reminded of how God continually works in my life.

I envision that these final pages of your study of Luke will serve a similar purpose in your life. These "take-away truths" have come as you have faithfully interacted with the life of Christ in the living Word of God and have observed His passion and purpose. What follows will be a record of your thoughts and responses to the Savior. Don't fail to complete this important final step of each lesson. Don't fail to take God's Word to heart. Don't fail to learn all you can about what it means to live with passion and purpose.

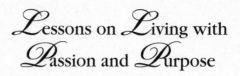

Lessons on Living with Passion and Purpose

Chapter	Take-Away Truths or Responses
1.	
2.	
3.	
4.	
5.	
6.	

7.

8.

9.

10.

11.

12.

13.

14.

15.

16.

17.

18.

19.

20.

21.

22.

23.

24.

Leading a Bible Study Discussion Group

What a privilege it is to lead a Bible study! And what joy and excitement await you as you delve into the Word of God and help others to discover its life-changing truths. If God has called you to lead a Bible study group, I know you'll be spending much time in prayer and planning and giving much thought to being an effective leader. I also know that taking the time to read through the following tips will help you to navigate the challenges of leading a Bible study discussion group and enjoying the effort and opportunity.

The Leader's Roles

As a Bible study group leader, you'll find your role changing back and forth from *expert* to *cheerleader* to *lover* to *referee* during the course of a session.

Since you're the leader, group members will look to you to be the *expert* guiding them through the material. So be well prepared. In fact, be over-prepared so that you know the material better than any group member does. Start your study early in the week and let its message simmer all week long. (You might even work several lessons ahead so that you have in mind the big picture and the overall direction of the study.) Be ready to share some additional gems that your group members wouldn't have discovered on their

145

own. That extra insight from your study time—or that comment from a wise Bible teacher or scholar, that clever saying, that keen observation from another believer, and even an appropriate joke—adds an element of fun and keeps Bible study from becoming routine, monotonous, and dry.

Second, be ready to be the group's *cheerleader*. Your energy and enthusiasm for the task at hand can be contagious. It can also stimulate people to get more involved in their personal study as well as in the group discussion.

Third, be the *lover*, the one who shows a genuine concern for the members of the group. You're the one who will establish the atmosphere of the group. If you laugh and have fun, the group members will laugh and have fun. If you hug, they will hug. If you care, they will care. If you share, they will share. If you love, they will love. So pray every day to love the women God has placed in your group. Ask Him to show you how to love them with His love.

Finally, as the leader, you'll need to be the *referee* on occasion. That means making sure everyone has an equal opportunity to speak. That's easier to do when you operate under the assumption that every member of the group has something worthwhile to contribute. So, trusting that the Lord has taught each person during the week, act on that assumption.

Expert, cheerleader, lover, and referee—these four roles of the leader may make the task seem overwhelming. But that's not bad if it keeps you on your knees praying for your group.

A Good Start

Beginning on time, greeting people warmly, and opening in prayer gets the study off to a good start. Know what you want to have happen during your time together and make sure those things get done. That kind of order means comfort for those involved.

Establish a format and let the group members know what that format is. People appreciate being in a Bible study that focuses on the Bible. So keep the discussion on the topic and move the group through the questions. Tangents are often hard to avoid—and even harder to rein in. So be sure to focus on the answers to questions about the specific passage at hand. After all, the purpose of the group is Bible study!

Finally, as someone has accurately observed, "Personal growth is one of the by-products of any effective small group. This growth is achieved when people are recognized and accepted by others. The more friendliness, mutual trust, respect, and warmth exhibited, the more likely that the member will find pleasure in the group, and, too, the more likely she will work hard toward the accomplishment of the group's goals. The effective leader will strive to reinforce desirable traits" (source unknown).

A Dozen Helpful Tips

Here is a list of helpful suggestions for leading a Bible study discussion group:

1. Arrive early, ready to focus fully on others and give of yourself. If you have to do any last-minute preparation, review, re-grouping, or praying, do it in the car. Don't dash in, breathless, harried, late, still tweaking your plans.

2. Check out your meeting place in advance. Do you have everything you need—tables, enough chairs, a blackboard, hymnals if you plan to sing, coffee, etc.?

3. Greet each person warmly by name as she arrives. After all, you've been praying for these women all week long, so let each VIP know that you're glad she's arrived.

4. Use name tags for at least the first two or three weeks.

5. Start on time no matter what—even if only one person is there!

6. Develop a pleasant but firm opening statement. You might say, "This lesson was great! Let's get started so we can enjoy all of it!" or "Let's pray before we begin our lesson."

7. Read the questions, but don't hesitate to reword them on occasion. Rather than reading an entire paragraph of instructions, for instance, you might say, "Question 1 asks us to list some ways that Christ displayed humility. Lisa, please share one way Christ displayed humility."

8. Summarize or paraphrase the answers given. Doing so will keep the discussion focused on the topic, eliminate digressions, help avoid or clear up any misunderstandings of the text, and keep each group member aware of what the others are saying.

9. Keep moving and don't add any of your own questions to the discussion time. It's important to get through the study guide questions. So if a cut-and-dried answer is called for, you don't need to comment with anything other than a "thank you." But when the question asks for an opinion or an application (for instance, "How can this truth help us in our marriages?" or "How do *you* find time for your quiet time?"), let all who want to contribute.

10. Affirm each person who contributes, especially if the contribution was very personal, painful to share, or a quiet person's rare statement. Make everyone who shares a hero by saying something like "Thank you for sharing that insight from your own life" or "We certainly appreciate what God has taught you. Thank you for letting us in on it."

11. Watch your watch, put a clock right in front of you, or consider using a timer. Pace the discussion so that you meet your cut-off time, especially if you want time to pray. Stop at the designated time even if you haven't

finished the lesson. Remember that everyone has worked through the study once; you are simply going over it again.

12. End on time. You can only make friends with your group members by ending on time or even a little early! Besides, members of your group have the next item on their agenda to attend to—picking up children from the nursery, babysitter, or school; heading home to tend to matters there; running errands; getting to bed; or spending some time with their husbands. So let them out *on time!*

Five Common Problems

In any group, you can anticipate certain problems. Here are some common ones that can arise, along with helpful solutions:

1. *The incomplete lesson*—Right from the start, establish the policy that if someone has not done the lesson, it is best for her not to answer the questions. But do try to include her responses to questions that ask for opinions or experiences. Everyone can share some thoughts in reply to a question like, "Reflect on what you know about both athletic and spiritual training and then share what you consider to be the essential elements of training oneself in godliness."

2. *The gossip*—The Bible clearly states that gossiping is wrong, so you don't want to allow it in your group. Set a high and strict standard by saying, "I am not comfortable with this conversation," or "We [not *you*] are gossiping, ladies. Let's move on."

3. *The talkative member*—Here are three scenarios and some possible solutions for each.

a. The problem talker may be talking because she has done her homework and is excited about something she has to share. She may also know more about the subject than the others and, if you cut her off, the rest of the group may suffer.

SOLUTION: Respond with a comment like: "Sarah, you are making very valuable contributions. Let's see if we can get some reactions from the others," or "I know Sarah can answer this. She's really done her homework. How about some of the rest of you?"

b. The talkative member may be talking because she has *not* done her homework and wants to contribute, but she has no boundaries.

SOLUTION: Establish at the first meeting that those who have not done the lesson do not contribute except on opinion or application questions. You may need to repeat this guideline at the beginning of each session.

c. The talkative member may want to be heard whether or not she has anything worthwhile to contribute.

SOLUTION: After subtle reminders, be more direct, saying, "Betty, I know you would like to share your ideas, but let's give others a chance. I'll call on you later."

4. *The quiet member*—Here are two scenarios and possible solutions.

a. The quiet member wants the floor but somehow can't get the chance to share.

SOLUTION: Clear the path for the quiet member by first watching for clues that she wants to speak (moving to the edge of her seat, looking as if she wants to speak, perhaps even starting to say something) and then saying, "Just a second. I think Chris wants to say something." Then, of course, make her a hero!

b. The quiet member simply doesn't want the floor.

SOLUTION: "Chris, what answer do you have on question 2?" or "Chris, what do you think about...?" Usually after a shy person has contributed a few times, she will become more confident and more ready to share. Your role is to provide an opportunity where there is *no* risk of a wrong answer. But occasionally a group member will tell you that she would rather not be called on. Honor her request, but from time to time ask her privately if she feels ready to contribute to the group discussions.

In fact, give all your group members the right to pass. During your first meeting, explain that any time a group member does not care to share an answer, she may simply say, "I pass." You'll want to repeat this policy at the beginning of every group session.

5. *The wrong answer*—Never tell a group member that she has given a wrong answer, but at the same time never let a wrong answer go by.

SOLUTION: Either ask if someone else has a different answer or ask additional questions that will cause the right answer to emerge. As the women get closer to the right answer, say, "We're getting warmer! Keep thinking! We're almost there!"

Learning from Experience

Immediately after each Bible study session, evaluate the group discussion time using this checklist. You may also want a member of your group (or an assistant or trainee or outside observer) to evaluate you periodically.

May God strengthen—and encourage!—you as you assist others in the discovery of His many wonderful truths.

Appendix
The Women in the Gospel of Luke

Luke, the writer, gives special consideration to women and to Jesus' ministry relationship to women. Throughout this Gospel account, Luke shows the importance of women in Jesus' life and work.

1:5-25	Elizabeth's background and the conception of John the Baptist are described.
1:26-38	Mary is introduced, and the angel Gabriel prophesies Christ's birth.
1:39-56	Mary and Elizabeth glorify God for the approaching birth of the Messiah.
1:57-66	Elizabeth's delivery of John the Baptist is recorded.
2:5-19	Mary treasures in her heart the events surround the birth of Jesus.
2:21-35	Simeon predicts Mary's suffering when the infant Jesus is presented at the Temple.
2:36-38	The prophetess Anna gives thanks to God for Jesus' birth.
2:41-51	Glimpses of Mary's role as a mother to Jesus are revealed.
4:25-26	Jesus refers to the widows in Israel in the days of Elijah.
4:38-39	Peter's mother-in-law is healed of a high fever.
7:11-16	The widow of Nain's son is brought back from the dead.
7:36-39	The woman who was a sinner anoints Jesus' feet.
8:1-3	Luke lists the women who supported Jesus'

ministry: Mary Magdalene, Joanna, Susanna, and many others.

8:19-21   Jesus' mother comes seeking Him.

8:41-56   Jesus heals a woman with an issue of blood and raises Jairus's daughter from the dead.

10:38-42   Jesus visits Mary and Martha's house.

11:27-28   A woman in the crowd speaks out to Jesus.

13:10-17   Jesus heals a crippled woman.

13:18-21   Jesus uses the daily practice of a woman baking bread to describe the kingdom of God.

15:8-10   Jesus uses a story of a woman searching for a lost piece of silver to illustrate God's joy over a repentant sinner.

18:1-8   Jesus uses a story of a woman who persisted before a judge to illustrate persistence in prayer to God.

21:1-4   Jesus notices and praises the sacrificial giving of a poor widow.

23:27-31   Jesus interacts with the daughters of Jerusalem who wept as He went to the cross.

23:49-56   The women who followed Jesus from Galilee continue with Him through the ordeal of His death on the cross and His burial.

24:1-11   Certain women are the first to observe the empty tomb of the resurrected Jesus (Mary Magdalene, Joanna, Mary, the mother of James, and other women).

Bibliography

Barton, Bruce B., David Veerman, and Linda C. Taylor. *Life Application Bible Commentary—Luke*. Wheaton, IL: Tyndale House Publishers, Inc., 1997.

Benware, Paul N. *Luke, the Gospel of the Son of Man*. Chicago: Moody Press, 1985.

Hendriksen, William. *New Testament Commentary—Exposition of the Gospel According to Luke*. Grand Rapids, MI: Baker Book House, 2002.

Jamieson, Robert, A.R. Fausset, and David Brown. *Jamieson, Fausset and Brown's Commentary on the Whole Bible*. Grand Rapids, MI: Zondervan Publishing House, 1971.

Luck, G. Coleman. *Luke, the Gospel of the Son of Man*. Chicago: Moody Press, 1970.

Pfeiffer, Charles F., and Everett F. Harrison, eds. *The Wycliffe Bible Commentary*. Chicago: Moody Press, 1990.

Notes

1. G. Coleman Luck, *Luke, the Gospel of the Son of Man* (Chicago: Moody Press, 1970), p. 9.

2. Ibid.

3. Ibid., pp. 10-11.

4. John MacArthur, *The MacArthur Study Bible* (Nashville: Word Bibles, 1997), p. 1531.

5. Herbert Lockyer, *All the Books and Chapters of the Bible* (Grand Rapids, MI: Zondervan Publishing House, 1966), p. 237.

6. MacArthur, *MacArthur Study Bible,* p. 1545.

7. Lockyer, *All the Books and Chapters of the Bible,* p. 237.

8. William Hendriksen, *New Testament Commentary—Exposition of the Gospel According to Luke* (Grand Rapids, MI: Baker Book House, 2002), p. 810.

9. Lockyer, *All the Books and Chapters of the Bible,* p. 238.

10. MacArthur, *MacArthur Study Bible,* p. 1555.

11. Lockyer, *All the Books and Chapters of the Bible,* p. 239.

12. "Christ Arose," written in 1874 by Robert Lowry.

13. Lockyer, *All the Books and Chapters of the Bible,* p. 240.

Personal Notes

Personal Notes

Personal Notes

BIBLE STUDIES *for* BUSY WOMEN

A WOMAN AFTER GOD'S OWN HEART® BIBLE STUDIES

*E*lizabeth takes women step-by-step through the Scriptures, sharing wisdom she's gleaned from more than 30 years as a women's Bible teacher.

Character Studies

Old Testament Studies

New Testament Studies

Understanding Your Blessings in Christ

NEW

EPHESIANS

Elizabeth George

About the Author

Elizabeth George is a bestselling author whose passion is to teach the Bible in a way that changes women's lives. She has more than 7 million books in print, including *A Woman After God's Own Heart*® and *A Woman's Daily Walk with God*.

For information about Elizabeth, her books, and her ministry, and to sign up to receive her daily devotions, and to join her on Facebook and Twitter, visit her website at:

www.ElizabethGeorge.com

Books by Elizabeth George

- Beautiful in God's Eyes
- Breaking the Worry Habit…Forever
- Embracing God's Grace Finding God's Path through Your Trials
- Finding God's Path Through Your Trials
- Following God with All Your Heart
- A Girl After God's Own Heart Devotional
- Heart of a Woman Who Prays
- Life Management for Busy Women
- Loving God with All Your Mind
- Loving God with All Your Mind DVD and Workbook
- A Mom After God's Own Heart
- A Mom After God's Own Heart Devotional
- Moments of Grace for a Women's Heart
- Quiet Confidence for a Woman's Heart
- The Remarkable Women of the Bible
- Small Changes for a Better Life
- Walking With the Women of the Bible
- A Woman After God's Own Heart®
- A Woman After God's Own Heart® Deluxe Edition
- A Woman After God's Own Heart®— Daily Devotional
- A Woman's Daily Walk with God
- A Woman's Guide to Making Right Choices
- A Woman's High Calling
- A Woman's Walk with God
- A Woman Who Reflects the Heart of Jesus
- A Young Woman After God's Own Heart
- A Young Woman After God's Own Heart— A Devotional
- A Young Woman's Call to Prayer
- A Young Woman's Guide to Making Right Choices

Study Guides

- Beautiful in God's Eyes Growth & Study Guide
- Finding God's Path Through Your Trials Growth & Study Guide
- Following God with All Your Heart Growth & Study Guide
- Life Management for Busy Women Growth & Study Guide
- Loving God with All Your Mind Growth & Study Guide
- Loving God with All Your Mind Interactive Workbook
- A Mom After God's Own Heart Growth & Study Guide
- The Remarkable Women of the Bible Growth & Study Guide
- Small Changes for a Better Life Growth & Study Guide
- A Wife After God's Own Heart Growth & Study Guide
- A Woman After God's Own Heart® Growth & Study Guide
- A Woman's Call to Prayer Growth & Study Guide
- A Woman's High Calling Growth & Study Guide
- A Woman Who Reflects the Heart of Jesus Growth & Study Guide

Children's Books

- A Girl After God's Own Heart
- God's Wisdom for Little Girls
- A Little Girl After God's Own Heart

Books by Jim George

- 10 Minutes to Knowing the Men and Women of the Bible
- The Bare Bones Bible® Handbook
- The Bare Bones Bible® for Teens
- A Boy After God's Own Heart
- A Husband After God's Own Heart
- Know Your Bible from A to Z
- A Leader After God's Own Heart
- A Man After God's Own Heart
- A Man After God's Own Heart Devotional
- The Man Who Makes a Difference
- A Young Man After God's Own Heart
- A Young Man's Guide to Making Right Choices

Books by Jim & Elizabeth George

- A Couple After God's Own Heart
- A Couple After God's Own Heart Interactive Workbook
- God's Wisdom for Little Boys
- A Little Boy After God's Own Heart

food by
Mark Sargeant

text by
Emily Quah

photographs by
Lisa Barber

Healthy Appetite

STERLING EPICURE
New York

STERLING EPICURE
New York

An Imprint of Sterling Publishing
387 Park Avenue South
New York, NY 10016

First Sterling edition 2012

First published in 2008 by Quadrille Publishing Ltd
Alhambra House, 27-31 Charing Cross Road
London WC2H 0LS

Food by Mark Sargeant
Text by Emily Quah

ISBN 978-1-4027-9788-0

Distributed in Canada by Sterling Publishing
c/o Canadian Manda Group, 165 Dufferin Street
Toronto, Ontario, Canada M6K 3H6

For information about custom editions, special sales,
and premium and corporate purchases, please contact
Sterling Special Sales at 800-805-5489 or
specialsales@sterlingpublishing.com.

Manufactured in China

2 4 6 8 10 9 7 5 3 1

www.sterlingpublishing.com